Physically Unclonable Functions (PUFs)

Applications, Models, and Future Directions

Synthesis Lectures on Information Security, Privacy, & Trust

Editors
Elisa Bertino, *Yahoo! Labs*
Ravi Sandhu, *University of Texas, San Antonio*

The Synthesis Lectures Series on Information Security, Privacy, and Trust publishes 50- to 100-page publications on topics pertaining to all aspects of the theory and practice of Information Security, Privacy, and Trust. The scope largely follows the purview of premier computer security research journals such as ACM Transactions on Information and System Security, IEEE Transactions on Dependable and Secure Computing and Journal of Cryptology, and premier research conferences, such as ACM CCS, ACM SACMAT, ACM AsiaCCS, ACM CODASPY, IEEE Security and Privacy, IEEE Computer Security Foundations, ACSAC, ESORICS, Crypto, EuroCrypt and AsiaCrypt. In addition to the research topics typically covered in such journals and conferences, the series also solicits lectures on legal, policy, social, business, and economic issues addressed to a technical audience of scientists and engineers. Lectures on significant industry developments by leading practitioners are also solicited.

Security and Trust in Online Social Networks
Barbara Carminati, Elena Ferrari, and Marco Viviani
2013

RFID Security and Privacy
Yingjiu Li, Robert H. Deng, and Elisa Bertino
2013

Hardware Malware
Christian Krieg, Adrian Dabrowski, Heidelinde Hobel, Katharina Krombholz, and Edgar Weippl
2013

Private Information Retrieval
Xun Yi, Russell Paulet, and Elisa Bertino
2013

Privacy for Location-based Services
Gabriel Ghinita
2013

Enhancing Information Security and Privacy by Combining Biometrics with Cryptography
Sanjay G. Kanade, Dijana Petrovska-Delacrétaz, and Bernadette Dorizzi
2012

Analysis Techniques for Information Security
Anupam Datta, Somesh Jha, Ninghui Li, David Melski, and Thomas Reps
2010

Operating System Security
Trent Jaeger
2008

Physically Unclonable Functions (PUFs): Applications, Models, and Future Directions
Christian Wachsmann and Ahmad-Reza Sadeghi

ISBN: 978-3-031-01216-7 paperback
ISBN: 978-3-031-02344-6 ebook

DOI 10.1007/978-3-031-02344-6

A Publication in the Springer series
SYNTHESIS LECTURES ON INFORMATION SECURITY, PRIVACY, & TRUST

Lecture #12
Series Editor: Elisa Bertino, *Yahoo! Labs*
             Ravi Sandhu, *University of Texas, San Antonio*
Series ISSN
Print 1945-9742   Electronic 1945-9750

Physically Unclonable Functions (PUFs)

Applications, Models, and Future Directions

Christian Wachsmann
Intel Collaborative Research Institute for Secure Computing at TU Darmstadt, Germany

Ahmad-Reza Sadeghi
Technische Universität, Darmstadt, Germany

*SYNTHESIS LECTURES ON INFORMATION SECURITY, PRIVACY, &
TRUST #12*

ABSTRACT

Today, embedded systems are used in many security-critical applications, from access control, electronic tickets, sensors, and smart devices (e.g., wearables) to automotive applications and critical infrastructures. These systems are increasingly used to produce and process both security-critical and privacy-sensitive data, which bear many security and privacy risks. Establishing trust in the underlying devices and making them resistant to software and hardware attacks is a fundamental requirement in many applications and a challenging, yet unsolved, task. Solutions solely based on software can never ensure their own integrity and trustworthiness while resource-constraints and economic factors often prevent the integration of sophisticated security hardware and cryptographic co-processors. In this context, Physically Unclonable Functions (PUFs) are an emerging and promising technology to establish trust in embedded systems with minimal hardware requirements.

This book explores the design of trusted embedded systems based on PUFs. Specifically, it focuses on the integration of PUFs into secure and efficient cryptographic protocols that are suitable for a variety of embedded systems. It exemplarily discusses how PUFs can be integrated into lightweight device authentication and attestation schemes, which are popular and highly relevant applications of PUFs in practice.

For the integration of PUFs into secure cryptographic systems, it is essential to have a clear view of their properties. This book gives an overview of different approaches to evaluate the properties of PUF implementations and presents the results of a large scale security analysis of different PUF types implemented in application-specific integrated circuits (ASICs). To analyze the security of PUF-based schemes as is common in modern cryptography, it is necessary to have a security framework for PUFs and PUF-based systems. In this book, we give a flavor of the formal modeling of PUFs that is in its beginning and that is still undergoing further refinement in current research.

The objective of this book is to provide a comprehensive overview of the current state of secure PUF-based cryptographic system design and the related challenges and limitations.

KEYWORDS

Physically Unclonable Functions (PUFs), physical security, embedded security, lightweight authentication, PUF-based remote attestation

Contents

Preface

Since embedded systems are deployed in many critical settings, their security, privacy, and safety aspects are of utmost concern. However, these systems are typically not protected against hardware attacks that aim at extracting the authentication secrets of these devices and to clone them. A general challenge for these systems is binding cryptographic protocols to the underlying hardware in a unique and unclonable way. In this context, Physically Unclonable Functions (PUFs) are a promising technology which exploits physical properties of hardware and can be integrated into cryptographic schemes. Since the introduction of PUFs in 2001 [91], researchers proposed many different PUF designs and a large variety of PUF-based security mechanisms. There are already some products using PUF technology in the market. PUFs were celebrated as promising primitives and many researchers investigated various aspects of PUFs including their design, implementation, and protocol integration as well as attacks on PUFs and PUF-based systems.

This book gives an introduction to PUFs and their integration into secure PUF-based cryptographic systems and security mechanisms. It explains the PUF concept and the state of the art of PUF-based protocol design on the example of PUF-based device authentication and remote attestation. The book gives insights into the formal modeling of PUFs, which is essential for the security analysis of PUF-based systems and still in its beginning.

We intend this book to be useful for students, active researchers, and practitioners. We hope that it serves as an introduction to PUFs and the design of secure PUF-based cryptographic schemes. Researchers starting their research on PUFs and PUF-based systems can use this book to familiarize themselves with the state of the art.

Parts of this book are based on Christian Wachsmann's doctoral dissertation [133]. Other parts are the result of joint collaborative research between the authors and our esteemed colleges and partners, including Frederik Armknecht, Anthony van Herrewege, Stefan Katzenbeisser, Ünal Koçabas, Farinaz Koushanfar, Joonho Kong, Vincent van der Leest, Roel Maes, Yossef Oren, Roel Peeters, Praveen K. Pendyala, Vladimir Rožić, Geert-Jan Schrijen, Heike Schröder, François-Xavier Standaert, and Ingrid Verbauwhede.

We thank Prof. Elisa Bertino for inviting us to write this book, Diane Cerra for supporting us in all organizational aspects, and Marina Blanton and Jorge Guajardo for their helpful comments.

Christian Wachsmann and Ahmad-Reza Sadeghi
December 2014

CHAPTER 1

Introduction

Embedded systems[1] are becoming pervasive and are massively used in many different areas of everyday life from medical, automotive and avionic industries to Industrial Internet (e.g., smart factories), and mobile infrastructures. A fundamental security requirement in these applications is the authentication and attestation, i.e., the ascertainment of the unique identity and integrity, of the underlying embedded systems. However, these systems typically have only limited computational and memory resources and do not provide sufficient protection, particularly against hardware attacks.

A fundamental challenge when using cryptographic schemes is securely storing the underlying cryptographic secrets. While most hardware security solutions, such as Trusted Platform Modules (TPMs) [121], do not scale to low-end embedded systems because of their high complexity and costs [2, 39, 73, 82, 117, 135], approaches that target low-end embedded devices do not consider physical attacks [26, 53, 79, 113]. In particular, cost-effective embedded systems often do not provide secure storage, which enables reading out cryptographic secrets through hardware attacks. A promising approach to protect these systems against hardware attacks are Physically Unclonable Functions (PUFs) [3, 66, 84]. PUFs are based on subtle physical differences of hardware components within production tolerances which can be easily measured but are infeasible to reproduce in practice. These differences are unique for each device and can be used as a means of identification, e.g., as a *physical fingerprint* of the device. This fingerprint can be used to generate cryptographic secrets and in cryptographic protocols. The main advantage of PUFs is that no secret needs to be securely stored. Instead, secrets are derived from the physical properties of the PUF when needed. This enables securely binding secrets and the software using them to the underlying hardware platform.

In the literature, many PUF-based authentication schemes have been proposed (see, e.g., [38, 83, 100, 122]). Most of them require a database of reference values for the verification of PUF fingerprints. This database can get very large, particularly because each reference value can be used only for one single authentication since otherwise replay attacks are feasible. Another, more practical approach derives cryptographic secrets from the PUF fingerprint, which are then used in standard cryptographic schemes. This requires the use of error correction codes to ensure reproducibility of the cryptographic secret derived from the PUF fingerprint.

---

[1]The term *embedded system* is widely used for a large variety of systems ranging from devices with minimal functionality to quite powerful systems such as smartphones and enterprise routers. In this book, we focus on low-end embedded systems with constrained resources.

The security of PUF-based cryptographic protocols is based on physical assumptions. In the literature, the security of PUF-based cryptographic schemes is usually analyzed in idealized PUF security models which do not consider all properties of PUF implementations. The first steps toward the development of a general formal security framework for PUFs implementations and PUF-based cryptographic schemes have been made.

In this book, we give insights into the usage of physical properties of hardware components for the design of secure cryptographic protocols that are suitable for a variety of embedded systems. The formal and practical solutions presented in this book address the fundamental challenge in information security of uniquely and unclonably binding cryptographic protocols to the underlying hardware. Specifically, the book discusses how PUFs can be integrated into cryptographic protocols on the example of PUF-based device authentication and remote attestation schemes that do not require to securely store any cryptographic secret in the embedded device, reducing the attack vector. The security analysis of these schemes and the evaluation of the underlying PUF implementations, requires formal tools: an evaluation framework for PUF implementations and a security model for PUF-based cryptographic schemes. These tools enable the evaluation of security-relevant properties of PUF implementations and the security analysis of PUF-based security mechanisms as it is common sense in modern cryptography.

BOOK OVERVIEW

We first give an introduction to Physically Unclonable Functions (PUFs) in Chapter 2, presenting the general PUF concept, the alleged properties of PUFs, and the most popular electronic PUF types and designs. We give an overview of the state of the art of attacks on PUFs and PUF-based systems in Chapter 3 and discuss advanced PUF concepts in Chapter 4. We investigate the properties of PUF implementations in Chapter 5, which presents the results of a large-scale security evaluation of implementations of the five most popular electronic PUF types in application-specific integrated circuits (ASICs), including Arbiter, Ring Oscillator, SRAM, Flip-flop, and Latch PUFs. We demonstrate the design of PUF-based cryptographic protocols on the example of device authentication and remote attestation in Chapter 6. The PUF-based authentication scheme enables scalable device authentication, is resistant to attacks that emulate the underlying PUF, and allows for extremely lightweight implementations on embedded devices. The PUF-based attestation scheme provides assurance of both the *identity* of the attested device and the *integrity* of its program memory content. In Chapter 7, we give insights into formalizing the most important security properties of PUFs and PUF-based systems, which is fundamental for the security analysis of PUF-based cryptographic protocols. Finally, we point out open research questions related to the design of scalable, efficient, and secure PUF-based cryptographic schemes and conclude in Chapter 8.

CHAPTER 2

Basics of Physically Unclonable Functions

Physically Unclonable Functions (PUFs) are increasingly proposed as central building blocks in cryptographic protocols and security architectures. Among others, PUFs enable unique device identification and authentication [83, 89, 99, 122], binding software to hardware platforms [25, 31, 33, 57], and secure storage of cryptographic secrets [62, 131]. Furthermore, they can be integrated into cryptographic algorithms [4] and remote attestation protocols [103]. Today, PUF-based security products are already announced for the market, mainly targeting IP-protection and anti-counterfeiting applications as well as radio-frequency identification (RFID) systems [44, 80, 128].

2.1 PUF CONCEPT, PROPERTIES, AND ASSUMPTIONS

A Physically Unclonable Function (PUF) is a noisy function that is embedded into a physical object, such as an integrated circuit (IC) [3, 66, 84]. When queried with a *challenge x*, a PUF generates a *response y* that depends on both x and the unique device-specific intrinsic physical properties of the object containing the PUF. Since PUFs are subject to noise induced by variations of their operating conditions, such as supply voltage and ambient temperature variations, PUFs return slightly different responses when queried with the same challenge multiple times.

PUFs are typically assumed to be *robust, physically unclonable, unpredictable*, and *tamper-evident*, and several approaches to quantify and formally define their properties have been proposed (see [3] for an overview). Informally, robustness means that, when queried with the same challenge multiple times, the PUF returns a similar response with high probability. Physical unclonability demands that it is infeasible to produce two PUFs that cannot be distinguished based on their challenge/response behavior. Unpredictability requires that it is infeasible to predict the response to an unknown challenge, even if the PUF can be adaptively queried for a certain number of times. Finally, a PUF is tamper-evident if any attempt to physically access the PUF irreversibly changes its challenge/response behavior.

2.2 PUF TYPES

There is a variety of PUF implementations (see [66] for an overview). The most appealing ones for the integration into electronic circuits and the focus of this book are *electronic PUFs*, which can be easily integrated into semiconductors and come in different flavors. *Delay-based PUFs* are based on race conditions in integrated circuits and include Arbiter PUFs [59, 63, 83] and Ring Oscillator PUFs [30, 67, 116]. *Memory-based PUFs* exploit the instability of volatile memory elements, such as SRAM cells [31, 40], flip-flops [65, 127], and latches [57, 115]. Finally, *Coating PUFs* [123] use capacitances of special dielectric coatings applied to the chip implementing the PUF.

2.2.1   DELAY-BASED PUFS

Delay-based PUFs are based on signal delays within integrated circuits (ICs) that are the result of manufacturing variations. The general approach is to design two identical signal paths consisting of wires and transistors that in theory should generate the same signal delay. However, due to manufacturing process variations, the physical characteristics of both signal paths will be slightly different and thus, the actual signal delay of each path will deviate from the ideal delay. These delay differences can be measured directly, e.g., using an arbiter,[1] or one can measure their influence on other physical characteristics of the surrounding circuit, e.g., the oscillating frequency of a ring oscillator.

Arbiter PUFs

Arbiter PUFs, which have been first presented by Lim et al. [59, 61], are based on race conditions in integrated circuits (ICs). Specifically, Arbiter PUFs are based on two identically designed signal paths consisting of wires, N switching components, and an arbiter at the end of both paths (cf. Figure 2.1). The N switching components allow the signal paths to be configured according to

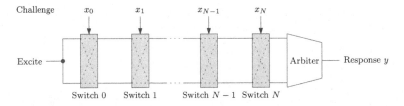

Figure 2.1: Basic Arbiter PUF design.

an external input $x = (x_0, \ldots, x_N)$, i.e., the PUF challenge. To evaluate the Arbiter PUF, both paths are simultaneously excited with the same signal. Depending on which of the two paths is faster, the arbiter generates output bit y which is used as PUF response. The delay caused by each signal path depends on the manufacturing variations of the transistors and wires of the switching components and their connections.

The delays of the signal paths are subject to varying operating conditions of the PUF, e.g., ambient temperature and supply voltage variations. However, the impact of these effects on the PUF response is minimized due to the the dual structure of Arbiter PUFs. More detailed, the de-

---

[1]An *arbiter* is a circuit designed to determine which of several signals arrive first.

lays of both signal paths are affected by very similar operating conditions whose effect is canceled out to a certain degree by the comparison of the arbiter. Note that in the case where the delay difference between both signal paths is below the setup time[2] of the arbiter, the resulting response bit y will be independent of the signal delays and determined only by the physical properties of the arbiter. This effect is called the *metastability* of Arbiter PUFs.

Arbiter PUFs can be efficiently implemented in application-specific integrated circuits (ASICs) [59, 61], while implementations on field-programmable gate arrays (FPGAs)[3] seem to be difficult due to the placing and routing constraints of the general FPGA hardware architecture [66]. Moreover, the delays caused by the individual components of the signal paths are additive, which enables model building attacks and emulating the challenge/response behavior of the PUF in software (cf. Section 3.1). To thwart these attacks, several modifications to the basic Arbiter PUF design have been proposed and are discussed in the following.

Lim et al. [61] presented the Feed-forward Arbiter PUF (cf. Figure 2.2), which, in addition to the PUF challenge $x = (x_0, \ldots, x_N)$, uses the output of intermediate arbiters to configure parts of the signal paths. This introduces non-linearities into the signal paths, which should mitigate

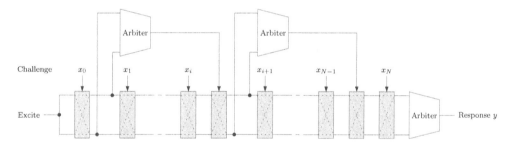

Figure 2.2: Feed-forward Arbiter PUF design.

basic model building attacks. However, this approach increases the metastability, which results in more errors in PUF response y. Moreover, Majzoobi et al. [70, 71] showed that Feed-forward Arbiter PUFs can be emulated. As a countermeasure, they propose the Lightweight Secure PUF [71] (cf. Figure 2.3) which is based on several interleaved Arbiter PUFs. More detailed, the challenge bits $x_0, \ldots, x_N$ of the overall PUF structure are permuted to generate different challenge bits for each of the underlying basic Arbiter PUFs. The overall PUF response $y = (y_0, \ldots, y_3)$ is generated by combining the response bits of the underlying Arbiter PUFs using XOR gates. However, Rührmair et al. [95, 96] showed that Lightweight Secure PUFs can be emulated using machine learning techniques (cf. Section 3.1).

Another approach to counter model building attacks [71] is based on the reconfigurability of FPGA hardware. The idea is to combine different Arbiter PUFs instances implemented on the

---

[2]The *setup time* is the minimum amount of time the input data signals should be held steady before the clock event (e.g., a rising clock edge) so that they can be reliably sampled.
[3]Field-programmable gate arrays (FPGAs) are integrated circuits (ICs) designed to be configured after manufacturing.

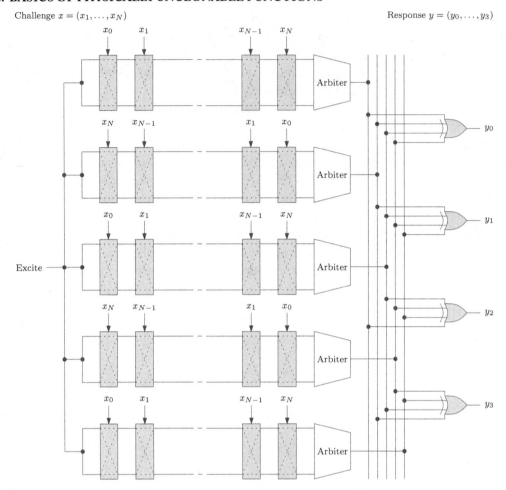

Figure 2.3: Lightweight Secure PUF Design (Example Based on Five Basic Arbiter PUFs).

same FPGA device as one single PUF. More specifically, some of the challenge bits are used to select the location of the Arbiter PUF on the FPGA which is then used to generate the response bits. Majzoobi et al. [71] use input and output networks that are difficult to invert to control the challenges and responses of the underlying Arbiter PUFs. However, it seems that this construction is susceptible to the model building attacks by Rührmair et al. [95, 96].

Ring Oscillator PUFs
Similar to Arbiter PUFs, Ring Oscillator PUFs exploit the delay differences in electronic circuits caused by manufacturing process variations. Ring Oscillator PUFs consist of several identically designed ring oscillators, which are loops of an odd number of inverters that, once stimulated,

oscillate at a certain frequency. The oscillation frequency of a ring oscillator can be measured using standard digital components. An edge detection circuit detects the rising edges of the output signal of the ring oscillator and increases a counter that counts the number of rising edges during a certain time period. The oscillation frequency of each ring oscillator depends on the the signal delays of its inverters and the connecting wires, which are affected by manufacturing process variations.

Basic Ring Oscillator PUF constructions do not support challenges. One approach to add support for challenges is to add controllable delay elements into the delay path of the ring oscillator (cf. Figure 2.4). An alternative Ring Oscillator PUF design uses the challenge to select two out

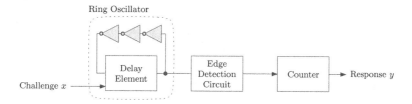

Figure 2.4: Ring Oscillator PUF design with controllable delay element.

of a set of ring oscillators and compares their oscillation frequencies. Similar to Arbiter PUFs, the delays in ring oscillator circuits are affected by operating conditions. Hence, the delay and thus the counter value is distorted and should not be used directly as PUF response. There are several approaches to reduce the effects of varying operating conditions on the responses of Ring Oscillator PUFs. Similar to Arbiter PUFs, the idea is to normalize the PUF response. This can be achieved by simultaneously evaluating two identically designed Ring Oscillator PUFs and then deriving the final PUF response by comparing their counter values (cf. Figure 2.5). Gassend et al. [28, 30] proposed using delay ratios, i.e., to divide one of the counter values by the other, to derive the final PUF response. Maes et al. [65] later showed that this construction creates a high correlation between the responses of *different* Ring Oscillator PUFs instances on *different* FPGA devices to the *same* challenge, and between the responses of the *same* Ring Oscillator PUF instance on the *same* FPGA device to *different* challenges. This means that the approach by Gassend et al. [28, 30] does not achieve the unpredictability property (cf. Section 2.1). Another approach by Suh et al. [116] is to select two ring oscillators and compare their oscillation frequencies (cf. Figure 2.5). More detailed, two counters count the rising edges of the signals generated by two ring oscillators selected by PUF challenge x and, depending on which of the two counter values is larger, a single PUF response bit y is generated. Ring Oscillator PUFs have been shown [66, 95] to be susceptible to model building attacks (cf. Section 3.1).

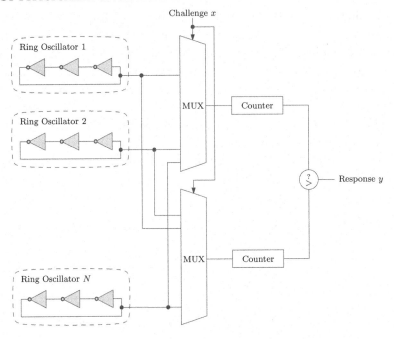

Figure 2.5: Ring Oscillator PUF design by Suh et al. [116].

ALU PUFs

ALU PUFs [55] exploit delay differences in identically designed and redundantly available logic components, such as the arithmetic logic units (ALUs)[4] in a processor. Similar to the Arbiter PUF [30], the ALU PUF exploits the time difference of the same signal traveling along two symmetric paths. These paths are identical by design and shall be the same by construction (layout), yet they incur different delays in practice due to manufacturing process variations. The ALU PUF design is shown in Figure 2.6 at the example of two 4-bit arithmetic logic units (ALUs). ALUs consist of integrated circuits (ICs) for computing arithmetic and logic functions in hardware. In the example, each ALU takes multiple input signals $x = (x_0, \ldots, x_7)$ (representing the ALU PUF challenge), guides them through a network of gates and wires (representing delay paths), and generates output signals $o = (o_1, \ldots, o_3)$ and $o' = (o'_1, \ldots, o'_3)$, respectively. Similar to the Arbiter PUF, the ALU PUF response $y = (y_0, \ldots, y_3)$ is generated by arbiters depending on which ALU's output signals arrive first. To ensure that both ALUs are stimulated with the same input signals at exactly the same time, a simple synchronization logic is used. Hence, the ALUs are utilized both as ALU *and* as PUF by only requiring a small hardware overhead (i.e., flip-flops and synchronization logic). Depending on the operand bit-length of the adders in the ALU, one can easily build ALU PUFs with an arbitrary number of response bits.

[4]An *arithmetic logic unit* (ALU) is a digital circuit that performs integer arithmetic and logical operations.

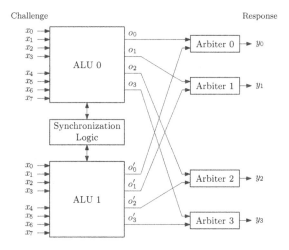

Figure 2.6: ALU PUF design (Example for 4-Bit ALUs) [55].

Response Verification of Delay-based PUFs

There are two approaches to verify the responses of delay-based PUFs: (1) using a database of challenge/response pairs (CRPs) recorded before deployment of the PUF, and (2) using an emulation **PUF.Emulate**() of the PUF based on a model of the delay-based PUF [68] (e.g., gate-level delay table lookups and delay additions; cf. Section 4.2). The drawback of the database approach is its limited scalability since it requires storing a large number of CRPs for each PUF implementation. Further, due to the limited size of the database, this approach allows only for a limited number of authentications since CRPs should not be re-used to prevent replay attacks. The emulation-based approach overcomes these drawbacks but requires a protected interface to read out the gate-level delays for emulating the PUF. This interface should be accessible only to a trusted entity (e.g., the PUF manufacturer) since otherwise the adversary could read out the gate delays and efficiently emulate the PUF, which would violate the unpredictability property. One approach to realize this interface for PUF implementations in ASICs is to provide a test interface that can be permanently disabled, e.g., by using fuses.

2.2.2   MEMORY-BASED PUFS

Memory-based PUFs exploit the power-up behavior of volatile memory cells and can be based on different memory technologies, including SRAM, flip-flops, and latches. These memory cells are inherently instable circuits that, by applying an external data signal input, can enter one of two different stable states to store one bit of information. A cell that is powered up *without* providing any data signal to it is an *uninitialized* memory cell. The state an uninitialized cell enters depends on the physical properties of its transistors, which are determined by manufacturing process variations. While most uninitialized cells preferably enter the same state ("0" or "1") after each power-up, some of them enter a random state each time. Note that the amount of unique responses of a memory-based PUF is limited by the number of its memory cells, i.e., the size of the underlying memory block.

SRAM PUFs

PUFs based on static random-access memory (SRAM) have been simultaneously and independently proposed by Guajardo et al. [31] and Holcomb et al. [40]. The challenge to an SRAM PUF is a memory address, while the corresponding PUF response is the content of the uninitialized memory cells at this address. An SRAM cell consists of two cross-coupled inverters and two additional transistors that are used to read and write data to the memory cell (cf. Figure 2.7). The

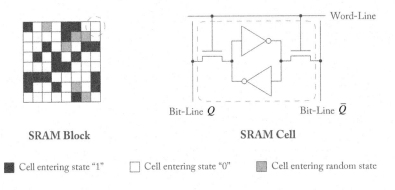

SRAM Block   **SRAM Cell**

■ Cell entering state "1"   □ Cell entering state "0"   ▨ Cell entering random state

Figure 2.7: SRAM PUF design.

information stored in the cell corresponds to one of the two stable states this circuit can enter. Both inverters are designed to be identical for optimizing the write performance of the memory cell. However, due to manufacturing process variations, the layout of the inverters is slightly different.

When an SRAM cell is powered without applying a data signal, the state the cell enters depends on the threshold voltage differences of its transistors. SRAM cells with large threshold voltage differences always enter either the "0" or the "1" state on each power-up. For SRAM cells with small threshold voltage differences the state entered is determined by the current operating conditions of the cell. In practice this means that some SRAM cells preferably enter the "0" state, others the "1" state, and some show no real preference and enter any of the two states with about the same probability. These three types of SRAM cells are randomly distributed over the array of memory cells that form the SRAM block. Those cells that always enter the same state can be used to create a unique and device-specific fingerprint.

The properties of SRAM-based PUFs have been evaluated for implementations based on FPGAs with dedicated SRAM blocks [31, 32] and ASICs such as dedicated SRAM chips and SRAM embedded into micro-controllers [40]. Note that SRAM PUFs cannot be implemented on every FPGA since most FPGAs automatically initialize the SRAM after power-up, i.e., they write zeros or ones to all the memory cells, which destroys the random start-up pattern used by SRAM PUFs. Moreover, to read the response form an SRAM PUF, the SRAM must be powered down and up again. Clearly, this can be problematic when the PUF must be evaluated while the chip containing the PUF is running and the SRAM is also used for other purposes by the device containing the PUF.

Flip-flop and Latch PUFs

PUFs based on flip-flops and latches use the same physical effects as SRAM PUFs but provide several advantages, including better integration on FPGA devices and resistance to hardware attacks. The Butterfly PUF [57] consists of a pair of cross-coupled latches that has two stable states and can be used to store one bit of information. However, the Butterfly PUF requires carefully designed dedicated circuitry. The FF PUF [65] is based on the same working principle as the Butterfly PUF but uses the existing flip-flops circuitry available in FPGA devices. Similar to SRAM cells, uninitialized flip-flops are in an undefined state that is determined by manufacturing process variations and that can be used as PUF response. The state of these flip-flops can be copied into the configuration memory[5] of the FPGA which can be read out from the FPGA over a configuration interface. The advantage of the FPGA-based Flip-flop PUF is that the underlying flip-flops are already present in the FPGA architecture and no additional hardware or configuration of the FPGA device is required. In contrast to SRAM PUFs, Flip-flop PUFs can be easily spread over the whole FPGA circuit and the location of the individual flip-flops can be obfuscated [127]. This seems to increase the difficulty of reverse-engineering and invasive hardware attacks against Flip-flop PUFs.

Latch PUFs have been proposed by Su et al. [114] in the context of device identification. Similar to flip-flops, latches are circuits with two stable states that can be used to store one bit of information. The difference between a latch and a flip-flop is that a latch does not require a clock signal, whereas a flip-flop always does. The working principle of Latch PUFs is the same as of SRAM PUFs and Flip-flop PUFs. Small threshold voltage differences of the transistors of the latch caused by manufacturing process variations lead to a mismatch. Hence, the state of the latch and thus the value it stores directly after power-up depend on the manufacturing process variations.

Flash-based PUFs

While all previously described memory-based PUFs are based on volatile memory, the Flash-based PUF [132] is based on non-volatile memory. Flash memory can be electrically erased and reprogrammed. Each memory cell is based on a transistor with two gates: the *control gate* and the *floating gate*. Charging the floating gate affects the resistivity of the transistor, which allows to store a logical "0" (floating gate charged, high resistivity) or "1" (floating gate not charged,

---

[5]The *configuration memory* of an FPGA contains *configuration data* that determines the functional behavior of the FPGA hardware. The configuration data is typically loaded into the configuration memory over a *configuration interface* while the FPGA device is booted.

low resistivity). The time needed to charge/discharge the floating gate such that the memory cell changes its logical state depends on the physical properties of the transistor, which are mainly determined by manufacturing variations. Since these times seem to be unique for each Flash memory device, they can be used to generate device-specific fingerprints.

2.2.3   COATING PUFS

Coating PUFs [123] are based on capacitances of protective coatings covering the top of integrated circuits (ICs). These capacitances are measured by several sensors placed below the coating of the chip. In contrast to standard protective coatings, the coating of Coating PUFs must be doped with dielectric particles of random size, shape, and location. This adds randomness to the PUF such that its challenge/response behavior depends on the variations of the manufacturing and doping processes. The chemical and mechanical properties of the coating provide tamper-evidence, which ensures that any attempt to physically or chemically tamper with the PUF permanently changes the capacitance of the coating and thus, the challenge/response behavior of the PUF. Moreover, measuring the capacitance of the coating from outside the chip yields different results than a measurement by the PUF sensors in the chip since capacitance measurements strongly depend on the exact sensor locations. Hence, the interface to the Coating PUF is protected against invasive hardware attacks, which means that the PUF responses are only accessible within the chip. This property is particularly important for applications where the PUF is used to securely store a cryptographic secret [62, 131]. Moreover, Coating PUFs can be used to protect other digital components in the integrated circuit (integrated circuit) against invasive hardware attacks. However, they do not protect against side-channel attacks or invasive attacks that physically attack the chip from its back, i.e., through the silicon layer. Typically, there is no challenge to a Coating PUF.

2.2.4   NON-ELECTRIC PUFS

Besides electric PUFs there are many other PUF types that are not based on electric effects, including optical, mechanical, and acoustic effects. However, these PUFs typically cannot be easily integrated into integrated circuits (ICs) since they often require non-standard manufacturing processes or special hardware components. Specifically, most non-electric PUFs require an external evaluation setup to measure the PUF response. An overview and more details on some non-electric PUFs can be found in the survey by Maes et al. [66].

2.3   NOISE COMPENSATION AND PRIVACY AMPLIFICATION

Many PUF-based applications require PUF responses to be reliably reproducible while at the same time being unpredictable [3, 4, 66]. However, since PUFs are inherently noisy and their responses are not uniformly random, they are typically combined with *fuzzy extractors* [22, 23].

Fuzzy extractors consist of a *secure sketch*, which is an algorithm that maps similar PUF responses to the same value (noise compensation or error correction) and a *randomness extractor* that extracts full-entropy bit strings from PUF responses (privacy amplification).

Enrolment Phase	Reconstruction Phase
Generate helper data h . . .	*. . . that is later used to recreate K.*
$y \leftarrow \mathsf{PUF}(x)$	$y' \leftarrow \mathsf{PUF}(x)$
$(K, h) \leftarrow \mathsf{FEGen}(y)$	$K \leftarrow \mathsf{FERep}(y', h)$
Store (x, h)	

Figure 2.8: Fuzzy extractor concept.

Fuzzy extractors and secure sketches generally work in two phases (cf. Figure 2.8). In the *enrolment phase* an algorithm FEGen computes some helper data h and a uniform bit string K (that could be used as cryptographic secret) from PUF response y to challenge x. Later, in the *reconstruction phase*, an algorithm FERep recovers K from helper data h and a distorted PUF response $y' = y + e$ to challenge x, where e is some error caused by varying operating conditions. An important property of fuzzy extractors and secure sketches is that one single helper data h can be stored and transferred publicly without disclosing the full PUF response y or K [23].

One limitation of fuzzy extractors and secure sketches with regard to their deployment in embedded systems is that the underlying error decoding algorithms are typically complex and require a large number of gates or long execution times [12, 23]. One approach to overcome this problem are *reverse fuzzy extractors* [38], which allow for very compact and fast implementations of secure sketches and fuzzy extractors. Reverse fuzzy extractors use the much more efficient helper data generation algorithm FEGen on the PUF-enabled device and the computationally intensive reproduction algorithm FERep is moved to the typically more powerful verifier (cf. Figure 2.9). As a consequence, a new helper data h is generated each time the PUF is queried and the verifier corrects reference value y from its database to the actual PUF response y', which is different each time the PUF is evaluated due to varying operating conditions.

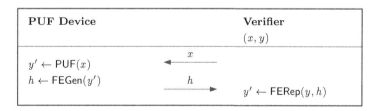

Figure 2.9: Concept of reverse fuzzy extractors.

There is one major pitfall of this approach that must be considered. Each execution of FEGen on a different noisy version of a PUF response to the same challenge reveals new helper data. However, secure sketches give no guarantee about the secrecy of the PUF response in the case where *multiple* helper data for different noisy variants of the same response are known [13]. Hence, reverse fuzzy extractors may leak the full PUF response, when FEGen and FERep are based on conventional fuzzy extractors. This is problematic in most PUF-based applications that require at least some bits of the PUF response to be secret. However, reverse fuzzy extractors can be securely implemented [38] based on the *syndrome construction* [23], which is a secure sketch with a highly efficient helper data generation phase and that has been shown [13] to be secure, even if multiple helper data for noisy variants of the same PUF response are known.

CHAPTER 3

Attacks on PUFs and PUF-based Systems

Theoretical works on Physically Unclonable Functions (PUFs) typically assume that the PUF cannot be emulated and that the PUF hardware is physically unclonable and tamper-resistant (cf. Section 2.1). However, it has been shown that most electrical PUFs can be efficiently emulated in software. Further, physical unclonability and tamper-resistance have not been sufficiently investigated and the security analysis of PUF implementations is subject of recent and ongoing research. In this chapter, we give an overview of the state of the art in attacking PUF implementations and PUF-based systems.

3.1 EMULATION ATTACKS

The number of responses of a memory-based PUF is limited by the number of its memory elements. This enables to read out all PUF responses and to emulate the PUF. Further, most delay-based PUFs are subject to emulation or model building attacks [59, 63, 70, 83, 95] which exploit the linear structure of existing delay-based PUFs to create mathematical models that allow estimating the response to a given PUF challenge. A number of countermeasures inserting non-linearity into the PUF's delay circuit have been proposed [59, 69–71]. However, Rührmair et al. [95] show that most of these approaches are ineffective against emulation attacks based on machine learning techniques, such as logistic regression and evolution strategies. The complexity of these attacks can be increased by obfuscating the actual PUF response using cryptography (cf. Section 4.1) [29] or XOR networks [69]. Emulation attacks have been shown to be effective against most delay-based PUFs, including Arbiter PUFs and Ring Oscillator PUFs (cf. Section 2.2.1).

3.2 SIDE CHANNEL ATTACKS

Side channel attacks are hardware attacks that aim to extract secret data, such as cryptographic secrets, from an electronic component. Hereby, the adversary observes the behavior (such as the power consumption, electromagnetic radiation, or timing behavior) of the component while it is using the secret data to be extracted. Since the behavior of the component is typically dependent on the data processed, it can leak information on this data. The fundamental observation is that processing a data bit of value "1" typically consumes a different amount of power or time than processing a data bit of value "0".

PUFs are typically used in combination with fuzzy extractors (cf. Section 2.3) and most PUF-based applications require PUF responses to be secret. Hence, side channel attacks against PUF-based systems typically target the fuzzy extractor to gather challenge/response pairs (CRPs) and other information that eases emulation attacks on the underlying PUF. Research on the side channel analysis of PUFs and fuzzy extractors has been recently started and there are only a few published results. Karakoyunlu et al. [47] and Merli et al. [74] show side channel attacks on implementations of common fuzzy extractors. Furthermore, Merli et al. [74] discuss potential side channel leakages of various PUF types. However, all known side channel attacks on PUF-based systems target the implementation of the algorithms processing the PUF responses, such as fuzzy extractors, and are independent of the underlying PUF construction.

3.3   FAULT INJECTION ATTACKS

Fault injection attacks aim to prompt erroneous behavior in a device by manipulating it in some way and, when combined with cryptanalysis, can lead to key recovery attacks. Faults may be injected in many ways, e.g., by operating the device under extreme environmental conditions or by injecting transient faults into specific components of the device.

Attempts to operate a PUF outside its normal operating envelope, e.g., by varying its supply voltage or ambient temperature, typically affect the challenge/response behavior and thus the robustness and unpredictability property of the PUF (cf. Section 5.3). Further, the impact of remanence decay effects[1] on the unpredictability and robustness of memory-based PUFs [41, 42, 101, 104, 119] enables denial-of-service and fault injection attacks to recover the PUF response. Recently, a fault-injection attack [81] based on the remanence decay in volatile memory has been shown, which allows launching a non-invasive cloning attack against SRAM PUFs.

Since implementations of fuzzy extractors (cf. Section 2.3) and the underlying error correction algorithms are typically not resistant to fault injection attacks and exhibit data-dependent behavior, fault injection attacks can cause unintended leakage of PUF-related secret information, such as cryptographic keys bound to the PUF. In particular, most fuzzy extractors are not secure in the case where the helper data can be modified by the adversary [13]. Thus, robust fuzzy extractors [22] should be used to prevent manipulations of the helper data.

3.4   INVASIVE ATTACKS

Invasive attacks typically aim at learning information on the cryptographic secrets stored in a device through analysis of the device hardware. This may include reverse engineering techniques

---

[1]The data written to volatile memory cells is typically not immediately lost after the cells are powered off but slowly decays over time.

and circumventing active protection mechanisms that should detect such attacks and react accordingly, e.g., by irreversibly deleting the secret stored in the device.

While a common assumption in the literature is that PUFs are tamper-evident or even tamper-resistant, this is not true for most known implementations of electronic PUFs. In fact some PUF types, such as SRAM PUFs, are resilient to influences of extreme operating conditions [49, 126] and physical tampering with the device containing the PUF [37]. This enables physically inspecting the PUF hardware and learning information that helps emulating the PUF [77]. Further, it has been shown [37] that after learning the response of an SRAM PUF p_1, a focussed ion beam (FIB) can be used to modify the circuits of the SRAM cells of another SRAM PUF p_2 so that p_2 shows a very similar challenge/response behavior as p_1.

Furthermore, the implementation of the algorithms and the circuits processing the PUF responses can be attacked [54, 118], e.g., by micro-probing the registers storing, the busses transferring, and the logic components processing the PUF responses in the device. One approach to protect these components against invasive attacks is encapsulating them in a tamper-evident PUF, such as the Coating PUF (cf. Section 2.2.3) [88, 123, 129].

CHAPTER 4

Advanced PUF Concepts

This chapter discusses advanced PUF concepts that enhance the security properties and extend the functionality of standard Physically Unclonable Functions (PUFs).

4.1 CONTROLLED PUFS

Most delay-based PUFs are subject to model building attacks that allow emulating the PUF (cf. Section 3.1). One approach to counter this problem are Controlled PUFs [30], which use cryptography in hardware to hide the actual PUF response from the adversary. Controlled PUFs typically apply a cryptographic hash function to the PUF challenges and/or responses, which introduces non-linearity and breaks up the link between the actual PUF response and the output of the controlled PUF. Clearly, this does not address the fundamental weakness of delay-based PUFs. Moreover, to maintain verifiability of the controlled PUF outputs, error correction must be applied before the PUF responses are processed by the cryptographic operation, which increases the complexity of the overall construction. Further, to protect against emulation attacks, the cryptographic component and the error-correction mechanism as well as their connecting wires must be protected against invasive and side channel attacks (cf. Sections 3.2 and 3.3), which may be hard to achieve in practice.

4.2 PUBLICLY VERIFIABLE AND EMULATABLE PUFS

The verification of PUF responses typically requires a database of reference challenge/response pairs (CRPs). This limits the scalability and efficiency of many PUF-based security mechanisms and can be a serious drawback in practice. Particularly, PUF-based cryptographic protocols would benefit form PUFs that can be verified without the need for a large CRP database.

One approach to counter this issue are publicly verifiable PUFs, which, similar to public-key cryptography, allow the verification of PUF responses based on a publicly known mathematical model of the PUF. The concept of publicly verifiable PUFs has been presented by Rührmair et al. [92–94] as SIMPL (Simulation Possible but Laborious) systems. A similar concept known as *public PUFs* has been independently presented by Beckmann et al. [7]. The idea of both concepts is that the PUF can be emulated in software using a mathematical model of the physical properties of the PUF hardware. However, this computation is assumed to take significantly more time than evaluating the actual PUF, which can be noticed by the verifier in a PUF-based protocol. This allows for the verification of PUF responses by any entity using the publicly available mathematical model of the PUF while preventing an algorithmic adversary from impersonating the PUF in the timeframe expected by the verifier. Concrete implementations of SIMPL systems have been presented by Rührmair et al. [94].

Another approach to remove the requirement of a CRP database are *emulatable PUFs* [35, 83]. In contrast to SIMPL systems and public PUFs, *emulatable PUFs* do not allow the public verification of PUF responses and assume the mathematical model of the PUF to be known only to authorized entities, such as the verifier in an authentication protocol. The security properties of practical instantiations of publicly verifiable and emulatable PUFs are still unclear and need further investigation.

4.3   RECONFIGURABLE PUFS

Most existing PUFs exhibit a static behavior while a variety of applications would benefit from the availability of PUFs whose characteristics can be changed dynamically, i.e., reconfigured, after deployment. For instance, PUF-based key storage [16, 28] and PUF-based cryptographic primitives [4] may require that previous secrets derived from the PUF cannot be retrieved any more (e.g., to achieve forward secrecy). Another example are solutions to prevent downgrading of software [58] by binding the software to a certain hardware configuration, such as a PUF, which requires the PUF behavior to be irreversibly altered upon installation of a software update.

Unfortunately, all known implementations of physically reconfigurable PUFs rely on optical mechanisms, reconfigurable hardware (such as FPGAs), or novel memory technologies [58, 71], which all have several limitations in practice. In particular, optical PUFs cannot be easily integrated into integrated circuits and require expensive and error-prone evaluation equipment. Further, FPGA-based solutions cannot be realized with non-reconfigurable hardware (such as ASICs), which is commonly used in practice [66]. Specifically, FPGA hardware usually is too expensive and complex for most embedded applications.

In this context, several attempts to emulate physically reconfigurable PUFs have been made. One of the first proposals was integrating a floating gate transistor into the delay lines of an Arbiter PUF, which allows physically changing the challenge/response behavior of the PUF based on some state maintained in non-volatile memory [61, 62]. Other approaches restrict access to the interface of the PUF and use part of the PUF challenge as reconfiguration data [58, 59], which, however, works only for certain PUF types. The concept of Logically Reconfigurable PUFs (LR-PUFs) has been presented and formalized by Katzenbeisser et al. [50]. In contrast to static PUFs, LR-PUFs can be dynamically reconfigured after deployment such that their challenge/response behavior changes in a random manner without replacing or physically modifying the PUF. The idea is amending a conventional PUF with a stateful control logic that transforms challenges x' and responses y' of the LR-PUF to challenges x and responses y of the underlying PUF (cf. Figure 4.1). The LR-PUF state needs not to be secret but it must be ensured that the adversary cannot set S to an old value. Although fault injection attacks against non-volatile memory (e.g., EEPROM or Flash) have been shown [111, 112], it seems to be difficult in practice to perform invasive attacks that change the content of specific non-volatile memory cells without affecting the content of the surrounding cells [112, 112]. Hence, in practice it should be infeasible for the adversary to write a specific value (e.g., an old LR-PUF state) into the non-volatile memory storing S. In particular, due to the increasing complexity of modern embedded systems and the fact that technology nodes are progressively getting smaller, the amount of precision and the quality of the equipment required to successfully perform such attacks renders them uneconomical in most practical applications (e.g., electronic ticketing). Furthermore, the adversary must not be able to manipulate the control logic such that it generates predictable states, which can be achieved by using a fault injection aware design [1, 75].

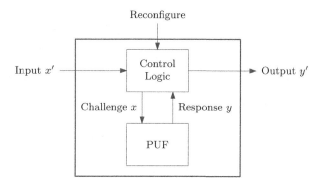

Figure 4.1: Logically Reconfigurable PUF (LR-PUF) concept.

CHAPTER 5

PUF Implementations and Evaluation

In contrast to most cryptographic primitives, whose security can be related to well-established (albeit unproven) assumptions, the security of Physically Unclonable Functions (PUFs) is assumed to rely on physical properties. The security properties of PUFs can either be evaluated theoretically, based on mathematical models of the underling physics [125, 129, 130] or experimentally by analyzing PUF instances built in hardware [34, 41, 43, 124, 127]. The first approach has the apparent drawback that mathematical models never capture physical reality in its full extent, which means that the conclusions on PUF security drawn by this approach are debatable. The main drawback of the experimental approach is its limited reproducibility and openness. Even though experimental results have been reported in the literature for some PUF implementations, it is difficult to compare them due to varying test conditions and different analysis methods. Furthermore, raw PUF data is rarely available for subsequent research, which greatly hinders a fair comparison.

In this chapter, we present one approach [49] to evaluate the most important properties (robustness and unpredictability) of PUF implementations for their integration into cryptographic primitives. This approach has been used for a large-scale security analysis of implementations of the five most popular electronic PUF types [49] in 65 nm ASICs, including different types and instances of delay-based PUFs (Arbiter and Ring Oscillator PUFs) and memory-based PUFs (SRAM, Flip-flop, and Latch PUFs). Since all these PUFs have been implemented in the same ASIC and analyzed with the same methodology, the results of this analysis allow for a fair comparison of the robustness and unpredictability of these PUFs. An independent analysis of electronic PUFs in 65 nm ASICs using a simpler evaluation methodology has been presented by Bhargava et al. [9].

5.1 PUF IMPLEMENTATIONS IN ASIC

The analysis presented in this section is based on data obtained from 96 application-specific integrated circuits (ASICs) that have been manufactured in 65 nm CMOS[1] technology. The ASIC has been designed within the UNIQUE research project by Intel, Intrinsic ID, and KU Leuven. Each ASIC implements multiple instances of three different types of memory-based PUFs (SRAM, Flip-flop, and Latch PUF) and two different types of delay-based PUFs (Ring Oscilla-

---

[1]CMOS is a technology for constructing integrated circuits (ICs).

Table 5.1: Physically Unclonable Functions (PUFs) implemented in the 96 ASICs

PUF Class	PUF Type	Number of PUFs per ASIC	Number of PUFs in all ASICs	Challenge Length (in Bits)	Response Length (in Bits)
Delay-based	Arbiter	256	24,576	2^{64}	2
	Ring Oscillator	16	1,536	$32,640 \approx 2^{15}$	2
Memory-based	SRAM	4	384	2^{11}	2^{32}
	Flip-flop	4	384	2^{8}	2^{32}
	Latch	4	384	2^{8}	2^{32}

tor and Arbiter PUFs). The main characteristics and the number of PUF instances in each ASIC are shown in Table 5.1. Furthermore, the ASIC is equipped with an active core that emulates the noisy working environment of a microprocessor. When enabled, this core continuously performs Advanced Encryption Standard (AES) [76] encryptions.

The implementation of the Arbiter PUF follows the basic approach presented by Lee et al. [59] and consists of 64 switch elements and an arbiter. The switch elements are connected in a line, forming two delay paths with an arbiter placed at the end (cf. Section 2.2.1). Each challenge corresponds to a different configuration of the delay paths. More detailed, each switch element has two inputs and two outputs and can be configured to map inputs to outputs directly (challenge bit "0") or to switch them (challenge bit "1"). During the read-out of the PUF response, the input signal propagates along both paths and, depending on which of the paths is faster, a single response bit is generated. To ensure that the delay difference results from the manufacturing process variations rather than the routing of the metal lines, a symmetric layout of the switch elements and full-custom layout blocks were used.

The Ring Oscillator PUF uses the design by Suh et al. [116] (cf. Section 2.2.1). Each Ring Oscillator PUF consists of 256 ring oscillators and a control logic which compares the frequency of two different oscillators selected by the PUF challenge. Depending on which of the oscillators is faster, a single response bit is generated. The individual ring oscillators are implemented using layout macros to ensure that all oscillators have exactly the same design, which is fundamental for the correct operation of the Ring Oscillator PUF.

The memory-based PUFs are implemented as arrays of memory elements (SRAM cells, flip-flops, and latches). All these memory elements are bi-stable circuits with two stable states corresponding to a logical "0" and "1". After power-up, each memory element enters either of the two states. The resulting state depends on the manufacturing process variations and the noise in the circuit. When challenged with a memory address, the PUF returns the 32 bit data word at that address. The implementations of the memory-based PUFs follow the SRAM PUF design by Holcomb et al. [41], the Flip-flop PUF design by Maes et al. [65], and the Latch PUF design by Su et al. [115] (cf. Section 2.2.2). Latch and Flip-flop PUFs are implemented using the standard cells from the 65 nm low-power library by TSMC[2]. The placement and implementation of the SRAM cells of the SRAM PUF has been done by TSMC's memory compiler. The Latch and

---

[2]Taiwan Semiconductor Manufacturing Company, Ltd.

Flip-flop PUFs are based on standard cells where all latches or flip-flops of the same PUF instance are grouped together in single block.

The test setup consists of a Xilinx Virtex 5 FPGA, a workstation, and an evaluation board which provides interfaces to interact with and to analyze the PUFs on the ASICs (cf. Figure 5.1). The evaluation board has been designed and manufactured by Sirrix AG, can take up to five PUF ASICs, and allows controlling the ASIC supply voltage with an external power supply. The

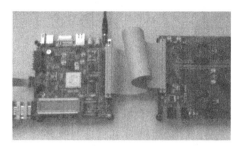

Figure 5.1: Test setup with Xilinx Virtex 5 FPGA (left) and evaluation board with five PUF ASICs (right).

interaction with the evaluation board and the ASICs is performed by the field-programmable gate array (FPGA), which is connected to the workstation that controls the PUF evaluation process and stores the raw PUF responses obtained from the ASICs. The tests at different temperatures have been performed in a climate chamber.

5.2 EVALUATION METHODOLOGY

Many PUF-based applications require PUF responses to be reliably reproducible while at the same time being unpredictable [3, 66]. Hence, the evaluation presented in this chapter focuses on the robustness and unpredictability properties of PUFs.

In the following, we denote with $HW(x)$ the Hamming weight of a bitstring x, i.e., the number of non-zero bits of x. With $HD(x, y)$ we denote the Hamming distance between two bit strings x and y, i.e., the number of bits that are different in x and y.

5.2.1 ROBUSTNESS ANALYSIS

Robustness is the property that a PUF always generates responses that are similar to the responses generated during the enrolment of the PUF. Note that PUFs should fulfil this property under different operating conditions, such as different ambient temperatures, supply voltages, and noise levels. The robustness of PUFs can be quantified by the bit error rate $BER := HD(y', y)/|y|$, which indicates the fraction of bits of a PUF response y' that are different from the response y observed during enrolment. Specifically, the maximum BER of all PUF instances in all ASICs is determined based on challenge/response pair (CRP) collected at different ambient temperatures

Table 5.2: Robustness test cases

Test Case	Active Core Off	On	Ambient Temperature $-40\,^\circ$C	$+25\,^\circ$C	$+85\,^\circ$C	Supply Voltage 1.08 V	1.2 V	1.32 V
E_1	×		×			×		
E_2	×		×				×	
E_3	×		×					×
E_4	×			×		×		
E_5	×			×			×	
E_6	×			×				×
E_7	×				×	×		
E_8	×				×		×	
E_9	×				×			×
E_{11}		×		×			×	

($-40\,^\circ$C to $+85\,^\circ$C), supply voltages ($\pm10\%$ of the nominal 1.2 V), and noise levels (active core enabled and disabled), which correspond to the corner values that are typically tested for consumer grade electronics. This shows the impact of the most common environmental factors on the BER of each PUF type. An overview of all test cases considered for robustness is given in Table 5.2. The BER of all PUFs in all ASICs has been estimated using the following procedure:

Step 1: Sample challenge set generation   A sample challenge set X' is generated for each PUF type (Arbiter, Ring Oscillator, SRAM, Flip-flop, and Latch PUF) and used in all subsequent steps. Note that all but the Arbiter PUF have a relatively small challenge space and hence, the whole challenge space of these PUFs can be used as sample set, i.e., $X' = X$. Since the Arbiter PUF has an exponential (in the number of its switch elements) challenge space, it has been tested only for a set X' of 13,000 randomly chosen challenges from X, which is a statistically significant subset of and representative for X.

Step 2: Enrolment   For each PUF instance, the response y_i to each challenge $x_i \in X'$ is obtained under nominal operating conditions (test case E_5) and stored as reference value in a database DB_0.

Step 3: Data acquisition   For all test cases E_p in Table 5.2, each PUF instance is evaluated 30 times on each $x_i \in X'$ and its responses are stored in a database DB_{E_p}.

Step 4: Analysis   For each PUF instance, the maximum bit error rate (BER) between its responses in DB_0 and its responses in each DB_{E_p} over all $x_i \in X'$ is computed.

5.2.2   UNPREDICTABILITY ANALYSIS

Unpredictability ensures that the adversary cannot efficiently compute the PUF response to an unknown challenge, even if he can adaptively obtain a certain number of other challenge/response pairs (CRPs) from the same and other PUF instances [3]. This is important in PUF-based applications, such as authentication protocols, where the adversary can forge the authentication

Table 5.3: Unpredictability test cases

Test Case	Active Core		Ambient Temperature			Supply Voltage		
	Off	On	$-40\,^{\circ}$C	$+25\,^{\circ}$C	$+85\,^{\circ}$C	1.08 V	1.2 V	1.32 V
E_{13}	×		×				×	
E_{14}	×			×			×	
E_{15}	×				×		×	
E_{16}	×			×		×		
E_{17}	×			×				×

when he can predict a PUF response. Unpredictability should be independent of the operating conditions of the PUF, which could be exploited by the adversary.

The unpredictability of a PUF implementation can be estimated empirically by applying statistical tests to its responses and/or based on the complexity of the best known attack against the PUF [3, 66]. Statistical tests, such as the DIEHARD [72] or NIST [98] test suite, can in principle be used to assess the unpredictability of PUF responses. However, since these test suites are typically based on a series of stochastic tests, they can only indicate whether the PUF responses are random or not. Moreover, they require more input data than the memory-based PUFs and Ring Oscillator PUFs in the ASICs provide.

Similar as in symmetric cryptography, the unpredictability of a PUF can be estimated based on the complexity of the best known attack. There are attacks against delay-based PUFs that emulate the PUF in software and allow to predict PUF responses to arbitrary challenges (cf. Section 3.1). These attacks are based on machine learning techniques that exploit statistical deviations and/or dependencies of PUF responses.

Another approach is estimating the entropy of PUF responses based on experimental data. In particular *min-entropy* indicates how many bits of a PUF response are uniformly random. The entropy of PUFs can be approximated using the context-tree weighting (CTW) method [134], which is a data compression algorithm that allows assessing the redundancy of bit strings [34, 43, 124, 127]. A more accurate approach to assess the unpredictability of PUFs is using Shannon entropy, which is a common metric in cryptography and allows establishing relations to other publications that quantify the unpredictability of PUFs using entropy [3, 41, 116, 125]. The analysis described in the following estimates the entropy and min-entropy of the responses of all PUFs in the ASICs and is more precise than previous approaches since it considers dependencies between the individual bits of PUF responses [49]. Furthermore, to get an indication of whether responses of *different* PUF instances are independent, the *inter-distance* [28, 30, 31, 59, 61, 114, 116, 123], i.e., the Hamming distance between the responses of *different* PUF instances is computed.

The unpredictability of all available PUFs has been assessed at different temperatures and supply voltage levels (cf. Table 5.3) to determine the effects of environmental variations on the unpredictability using the following procedure.

Step 1: Sample challenge set generation   For each PUF type, a sample challenge set X' is generated that is used in all subsequent steps. For all but the Arbiter PUF, the complete challenge space is used as a sample challenge set, i.e., $X' = X$. Since the Arbiter PUF has an exponential (in the number of its switching elements) challenge space, it is again tested only for a subset $X' \subset X$ of challenges that is statistically representative for the whole challenge set X. The subsequent analysis steps require $X' = \{x' \in X'' | \mathsf{HD}(x, x') \leq k\}$, which includes a set X'' of randomly chosen challenges and all challenges that differ in at most k bits from each challenge in X'' (which may be known to the adversary). The evaluation uses X'' consisting of 200 randomly chosen challenges from X and $k = 1$. Since the Arbiter PUFs in the ASICs use 64 bit challenges, in the evaluation X' consists of $64 \cdot 200 = 12,800$ challenges.

Step 2: Data acquisition   For all test cases E_q in Table 5.3, each PUF instance is evaluated on each $x_i \in X'$ and the responses y are stored in a database DB_{E_q}.

Step 3: Analysis   For each test case E_q, the responses in DB_{E_q} are analyzed as follows.

Step 3a: Entropy estimation   For each PUF instance, the entropy and min-entropy of all its responses in DB_{E_q} are estimated as detailed in the next paragraph.

Step 3b: Inter-distance   For each PUF type, the inter-distance, i.e., the Hamming distance $\mathsf{HD}(y, y')$ of all pairs of responses (y, y') in DB_{E_q} generated by pairwise *different* PUF instances for the *same* challenge x is computed. Note that the entropy estimation in the previous step considers only responses of the *same* PUF instance, while the inter-distances indicate whether responses of *different* PUF instances are independent. This is important to prevent the adversary from predicting the responses of one PUF implementation based on the challenge/response pairs (CRPs) of another (e.g., his own) PUF implementation, which would contradict the unpredictability property.

Details on Entropy Estimation
One approach to estimate the entropy of PUF responses is as follows. Let x be the PUF challenge for which the adversary should predict response y. Further, let $Y(x)$ be the random variable representing y. Moreover, let $W(x)$ be the random variable representing the set of all responses of the PUF except y, i.e., $W(x) = \{y' | y' \leftarrow \mathsf{PUF}(x'); x' \in X \setminus \{x\}\}$. When using y in cryptographic protocols, one is interested in the conditional entropy

$$\mathbf{H}(Y|W) = -\sum_{x \in X} \Pr\big[Y(x), W(x)\big] \cdot \log_2 \Pr\big[Y(x)|W(x)\big] \tag{5.1}$$

and the conditional min-entropy

$$\mathbf{H}_\infty(Y|W) = -\log_2\big(\max_{x \in X}\big\{\Pr\big[Y(x)|W(x)\big]\big\}\big), \tag{5.2}$$

which quantify the average and minimal number of bits of y, respectively, that cannot be predicted by the adversary, even in case all other responses in $W(x)$ are known. Hence, $2^{-\mathbf{H}_\infty(Y|W)}$ is an information-theoretic upper bound for the probability that the adversary guesses PUF response y to challenge x.

However, computing Equations 5.1 and 5.2 for $W(x)$ is difficult since (1) the sizes of the underlying probability distributions are exponential in the response space size and (2) the complexity of computing $\mathbf{H}(Y|W)$ grows exponentially with the challenge space size of the PUF to be analyzed. Hence, Equations 5.1 and 5.2 can at most be estimated by making assumptions on the physical properties of the PUF that reduce the size of $W(x)$.

Assumptions on memory-based PUFs   A common assumption on memory-based PUFs is that spatially distant memory cells are independent [3, 66]. A similar assumption has been used by Holcomb et al. [41], who estimated the entropy of SRAM PUF responses based on the assumption that individual bytes of SRAM are independent. However, physically neighboring memory cells can strongly influence each other, in particular when they are physically connected.[3] Hence, the entropy estimation should also consider dependencies between neighboring memory cells (which could be exploited by the adversary) while assuming that spatially distant memory cells are independent. More specifically, the entropy of PUF response bit $Y_{i,j}$ of the memory cell at row i and column j is computed under the worst case assumption that the values of all neighboring memory cells $W'(x) = (Y_{i-1,j}, Y_{i,j+1}, Y_{i+1,j}, Y_{i,j-1})$ are known. This means that Equations 5.1 and 5.2 are computed for $W'(x)$.

Note that the bit-pattern read from an SRAM may not correspond to its physical layout. This means that neighboring bits in the bit-pattern read from the SRAM may be stored in physically distant cells. Hence, before estimating the entropy using the described approach, the bit-patterns read from the SRAM must be reordered to match the physical layout of the SRAM cells.

Assumptions on Ring Oscillator PUFs   The Ring Oscillator PUFs in the ASICs compare the oscillation frequency of two ring oscillators O_i and O_j selected by PUF challenge $x = (i, j)$ and return a response $Y(i, j)$, depending on which of the two oscillators had the higher frequency. Since neighboring ring oscillators may affect each other (e.g., by electromagnetic induction), the potential dependency between the frequencies of neighboring oscillators is considered, while the frequency of spatially distant oscillators is assumed to be independent. Thus, Equations 5.1 and 5.2 are computed for $W'(i, j) = \left(Y_{i-2,j}, Y_{i-1,j}, Y_{i+1,j}, Y_{i+2,j}\right)$.

Assumptions on Arbiter PUFs   Arbiter PUFs measure the delay difference of two delay lines that are configured by the PUF challenge. The individual delays caused by the switches and their connections are additive, which implies that PUF response y to challenge x can be computed if a sufficient number of responses to challenges that are close to x are known. Hence, Equations 5.1

---

[3]SRAM cells are typically arranged in a matrix where all cells in a row are connected by a word line and all cells in a column are connected by a bit line.

and 5.2 are computed for $W'(x) = \{y' \leftarrow \mathsf{PUF}(x')|x' \in X,'' \; \mathsf{HD}(x, x') \leq k\}$, which corresponds to the worst case where the adversary knows responses to challenges that differ in at most k bits from the challenge which of the response he must guess. The evaluation in this chapter uses X'' consisting of 200 randomly chosen challenges from challenge set X and $k = 1$.

Computing the entropy   To compute the entropy and min-entropy (Equations 5.1 and 5.2) for each test case E_q, $\Pr\left[x = Y(x), w = W(x)\right]$ is first estimated for each $x \in X'$ by dividing the number of observations of each tuple (x, w) in database DB_{E_q} by the size of sample challenge set X'. Further, to compute $\Pr\left[x = Y(x)|w = W(x)\right] = \Pr\left[x = Y(x), w = W(x)\right]/\Pr\left[w = W(x)\right]$, $\Pr\left[w = W(x)\right]$ is estimated by dividing the number of observations of each tuple $(Y(x), w = W(x))$ in database DB_{E_i} by the size of X'. Eventually, these empirically estimated probability distributions are used to compute the entropy and min-entropy according to Equations 5.1 and 5.2, respectively.

5.3   EVALUATION RESULTS

The evaluation methodology described in Section 5.2 has been applied to all PUF instances in all ASICs. The results are illustrated using *bean plots* [46] which allow an intuitive visualization of empirical probability distributions (cf. Figures 5.2 to 5.4). Each bean shows two distributions, smoothed by a Gaussian kernel to give the impression of a continuous distribution, together with their means indicated by black bars. The distribution in black on the left side typically corresponds to data collected under normal PUF operating conditions, while the one in gray on the right side corresponds to some other test case in Tables 5.2 and 5.3. This allows an easy visualization of the PUF behavior under changing environmental conditions. Each plot contains several beans that correspond to the different PUF types available in the ASICs, which allows an easy comparison of the results for different PUF types.

5.3.1   ROBUSTNESS RESULTS

The bit error rate (BER) has been computed under varying environmental conditions (cf. Table 5.3). The results show that all Arbiter, Ring Oscillator, and SRAM PUF instances have a very similar BER, while there is a big variability in the BERs of the Flip-flop and Latch PUF instances (cf. Figure 5.2). Further, the BER of the Arbiter, Ring Oscillator, and SRAM PUF instances is below 10% for all test cases, which can be handled by common error correction schemes, such as fuzzy extractors (cf. Section 2.3). The BER of most PUFs depends on the operating temperature. Compared to $+25\,°C$ (test case E_5), at $-40\,°C$ (test case E_2) the BER of the Flip-flop and Latch PUF increases significantly, while the BER of the Ring Oscillator and SRAM PUF increases only slightly, and the BER of the Arbiter PUF hardly changes (cf. Figure 5.2-a). A similar behavior of BERs can be observed at $+85\,°C$ (test case E_8; Figure 5.2-b). All PUFs in all ASICs turned out to be robust against variations of their supply voltages. Compared to nominal operating conditions (test case E_5), the BERs only slightly increase when varying the supply voltage by 10% (test cases

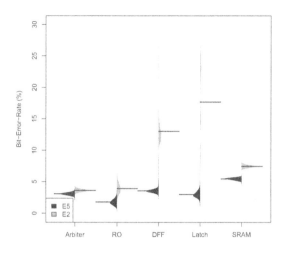

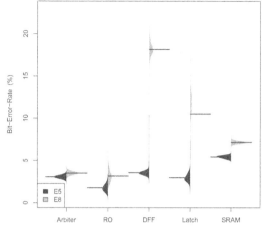

5.2-a BER at $+25\,^{\circ}$C (test case E_5, black) and at $-40\,^{\circ}$C (test case E_2, gray).

5.2-b BER at $+25\,^{\circ}$C (test case E_5, black) and at $+85\,^{\circ}$C (test case E_8, gray).

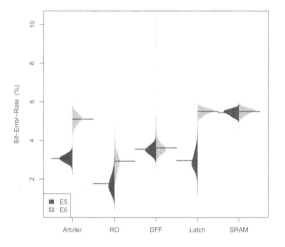

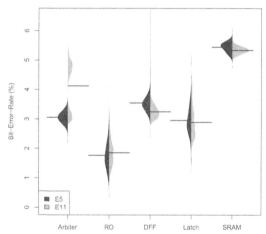

5.2-c BER at 1.20 V (nominal supply voltage, test case E_5, black) and at 1.32 V ($+10\%$ overvoltage, test case E_6, gray).

5.2-d BERs with active core off (test case E_5, black) and active core on (test case E_{11}, gray).

Figure 5.2: Distribution of the bit error rates (BERs) in percent over all PUF instances at different ambient temperatures, supply voltages, and noise levels.

E_4 and E_6; Figure 5.2-c). The Arbiter PUF exhibits a significantly increased BER when operated in a noisy working environment (test case E_{11}; Figure 5.2-d) while there is no significant change of the BER of all other PUFs. One observation is that the BER of those Arbiter PUF instances that are spatially close to the active core significantly changes, while those that are farther away are not directly affected, which can be seen on the two peaks of the gray graph of the Arbiter PUF in Figure 5.2-d.

5.3.2   UNPREDICTABILITY RESULTS

This section presents the results of the unpredictability analysis.

Entropy Estimation

The results of the entropy estimation described in Section 5.2.2 provide insights into the entropy and min-entropy of PUF responses (cf. Figure 5.3). The entropy of responses corresponding to neighboring Arbiter PUF challenges is remarkably low, which confirms the high prediction rate of emulation attacks on Arbiter PUFs reported in the literature (cf. Section 3.1) [95]. The entropy and min-entropy of the Ring Oscillator and SRAM PUF responses is invariant to temperature (test cases E_{13}, E_{14}, and E_{15}; Figures 5.3-a to 5.3-c) and supply voltage (test cases E_{16} and E_{17}; Figure 5.3-d) variations. Moreover, the entropy and min-entropy of Flip-flop and Latch PUFs vary with the operating temperature (test cases E_{13}, E_{14}, and E_{15}; Figures 5.3-a to 5.3-c) and are constant for different supply voltages (test cases E_{16} and E_{17}; Figure 5.3-d).

Inter-distances

The inter-distance test (cf. Section 5.2.2) gives an indication of whether the responses generated by different PUF instances to the same challenge are independent. The results show that, independent of the ambient temperature (test cases E_{13}, E_{14}, and E_{15}) and supply voltage (test cases E_{16} and E_{17}), the responses of different Ring Oscillator and SRAM PUF instances have the ideal inter-distance of 0.5, while there seem to be dependencies between the responses generated by different Arbiter PUF instances to the same challenge (cf. Figure 5.4). The inter-distance of the responses of the Flip-flop PUFs changes for different temperatures and supply voltages. At $+85\,°C$ (test case E_{15}; Figure 5.4-b) the inter-distance of the Flip-flop PUF is ideal, while it is biased toward zero at $-40\,°C$ (test case E_{13}; Figure 5.4-a). Moreover, at $1.08\,V$ (-10% undervoltage, test case E_{16}; Figure 5.4-c) a bias of the inter-distance toward one can be observed, while the inter-distance at $1.32\,V$ ($+10\%$ overvoltage, test case E_{17}; Figure 5.4-d) is similar to the distribution at nominal operating conditions (test case E_{14}). The inter-distance of the responses of the Latch PUFs is biased toward zero and invariant for different supply voltages.

5.3.3   DISCUSSION

The results show that Arbiter, Ring Oscillator, and SRAM PUFs are more robust to temperature variations than the Latch and Flip-flop PUFs. This could be due to the dual nature of these PUFs,

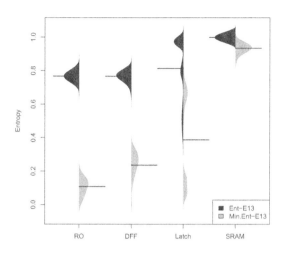

5.3-a Entropy (black) and min-entropy (gray) at $-40\,°C$ (test case E_{13}).

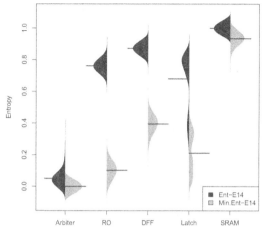

5.3-b Entropy (black) and min-entropy (gray) at $+25\,°C$ (test case E_{14}).

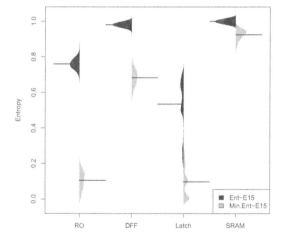

5.3-c Entropy (black) and min-entropy (gray) at $+85\,°C$ (test case E_{15}).

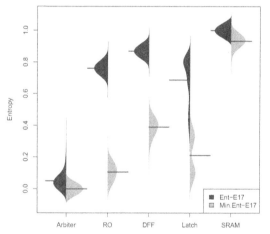

5.3-d Entropy (black) and min-entropy (gray) at $1.32\,V$ ($+10\%$ overvoltage, test case E_{17}).

Figure 5.3: Distribution of the entropy (black) and min-entropy (gray) over all PUF instances at different ambient temperatures and supply voltages. Note that the parts of the graphs showing an entropy/min-entropy < 0 and > 1 are drawing errors due to the Gaussian kernel used to smooth the discrete distributions to give the impression of a continuous distribution.

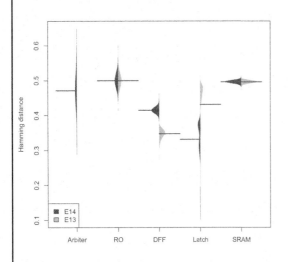

5.4-a Hamming distance at $+25\,^\circ$C (test case E_{14}, black) and at $-40\,^\circ$C (test case E_{13}, gray).

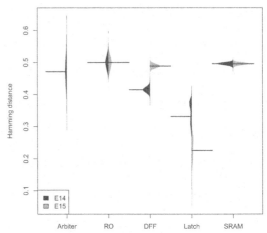

5.4-b Hamming distance at $+25\,^\circ$C (test case E_{14}, black) and at $+85\,^\circ$C (test case E_{15}, gray).

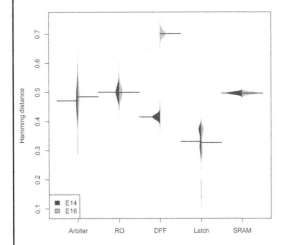

5.4-c Hamming distance at 1.20 V (nominal supply voltage, test case E_{14}, black) and at 1.08 V (-10% undervoltage, test case E_{16}, gray).

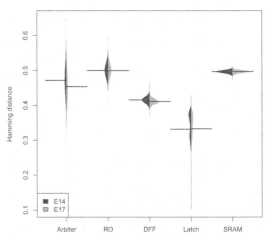

5.4-d Hamming distance at 1.20 V (nominal supply voltage, test case E_{14}, black) and at 1.32 V ($+10\%$ overvoltage, test case E_{17}, gray).

Figure 5.4: Distribution of the inter-distance (Hamming distance) over all PUF instances at different ambient temperatures and supply voltages.

i.e., the two delay paths, two ring oscillators, and the symmetrical structure of the SRAM cells, respectively. Standard cell libraries typically use implementations based on transmission gates, which are more compact than static latches or flip-flops with a dual structure and there is no duality or symmetry in their transistor schematics. Further, the results of the inter-distance test indicate that the unpredictability of PUFs with a dual structure is less affected by temperature variations.

Since the Arbiter PUF design is based on delay accumulation, it is very susceptible to emulation attacks (cf. Section 3.1). An example illustrating this fact is the case where two challenges differ in only the last bit. In this case, signals travel along the same path through 63 delay elements and only in the last element the path will be different. If the adversary knows the outcome for one challenge, he can guess the outcome of the other one with high probability, which might explain the low entropy and min-entropy of the Arbiter PUF responses.

5.4 SUMMARY

Arbiter PUF responses have a very low entropy and their use in applications with strict unclonability and unpredictability requirements should be carefully considered. Further, Arbiter PUFs are susceptible to changes of their supply voltage and to environmental noise, which significantly increases the bit error rate (BER) of their responses. However, the BER stays within acceptable bounds and can be compensated by error correction mechanisms.

Flip-flop and Latch PUFs are susceptible to temperature variations, which have a significant effect on the BER and the unpredictability of the PUF responses. Hence, Flip-flop and Latch PUFs should not be used in an environment where the adversary can lower the ambient temperature of the PUF, reducing the entropy of the PUF responses.

The SRAM and Ring Oscillator PUFs achieve almost all desired properties of a PUF: the BER does not change significantly under different operating conditions, the entropy of the PUF responses is high, and the responses generated by different PUF instances seem to be independent. However, the Ring Oscillator PUF exhibits a low min-entropy, which might be problematic in some applications. Hence, SRAM PUFs seem to be the most suitable choice for applications where the PUF is used to generate a secret, e.g., a cryptographic key.

CHAPTER 6

PUF-based Cryptographic Protocols

The classical application of Physically Unclonable Functions (PUFs) is the identification and authentication of physical objects, such as electronic devices. PUFs have been first proposed in the context of anti-counterfeiting solutions that prevent cloning (i.e., unauthorized copying) of products. There are many proposals to build identification and authentication schemes based on PUFs for various devices, mainly lightweight solutions that are applicable to resource-constrained embedded systems. PUFs can be used to securely bind secrets (such as cryptographic keys) to the physical characteristics of a device.

In this chapter, we discuss how PUFs can be integrated into cryptographic protocols on the example of PUF-based device authentication and PUF-based attestation. Device authentication aims at enabling a verifier to recognize which device it is communicating to and the (cryptographic) corroboration of the identity of a device. Attestation enables the verifier to get assurance of the integrity of the code and data residing on this device, which is a fundamental challenge in information security with high relevance to practice.

6.1 LIGHTWEIGHT AUTHENTICATION BASED ON PUFS

The common approach [11, 21, 89] to authenticate a PUF-enabled device is querying its PUF with a challenge from a pre-recorded database of challenge/response pairs (CRPs). The device is accepted only if its response matches a PUF response in the database. An alternative approach [99, 122] is using the PUF to generate the authentication secret of the device for use in a classical authentication protocol. However, both approaches have several drawbacks in practice: PUF-based key storage requires the device to reliably recover the (bit-exact) cryptographic secret from the noisy PUF response using some kind of error correction mechanism (cf. Section 2.3), whose implementation can be expensive in terms of the number of gates [12, 23]. Further, existing PUF-based authentication schemes are not scalable, allow only for a limited number of authentications, or are subject to replay, denial-of-service, or emulation attacks. More detailed, there is typically no support for mutual authentication between the device and the verifier; most PUF types are vulnerable to emulation attacks (cf. Section 3.1) and would allow emulating the device; some schemes are subject to denial-of-service attacks that permanently prevent devices from authenticating; and some schemes are not scalable and allow for only a limited number of authentication protocol-runs since they rely on a database containing a large number of CRPs of the PUF of each device. A practical PUF-based device authentication scheme should support an unlimited number of authentication protocol-runs, be resistant to emulation attacks, and should not require the verifier to store a large number of CRPs.

We first give an overview of existing PUF-based authentication schemes in Section 6.1.1. Then we show in Section 6.1.2 how PUFs can be used for device authentication on the example of a scalable and lightweight PUF-based authentication protocol for embedded devices [38]. This scheme supports mutual authentication of devices and verifiers and does not require the verifier to store a large number of CRPs. It uses reverse fuzzy extractors (cf. Section 2.3) and allows for a very compact implementation requiring only minimal resources on the device.

6.1.1 LITERATURE OVERVIEW OF PUF-BASED DEVICE AUTHENTICATION

One of the first proposals of using PUFs for lightweight authentication is by Ranasinghe et al. [89], who proposed the manufacturer of a PUF-enabled device $\mathcal{D}$ to store a set of CRPs in a database, which can later be used by verifiers to authenticate $\mathcal{D}$. The idea is that the verifier chooses a challenge from the database, queries the PUF of $\mathcal{D}$ and checks whether the database contains a tuple that matches the response received from $\mathcal{D}$. A limitation of this approach is that CRPs cannot be re-used since this would enable replay attacks and allow tracing of $\mathcal{D}$. Hence, the number of device authentications is limited by the number of CRPs in the database. This scheme has been implemented based on Arbiter PUFs [21]. A similar approach based on the physical characteristics of SRAM cells has been proposed by Holcomb et al. [40]. Another approach to PUF-based authentication [11] aims at preventing unauthorized tracking of devices. A major drawback of this scheme is that devices can be authenticated only a limited number of times without being re-initialized, which enables denial-of-service attacks.

A privacy-preserving PUF-based authentication scheme has been presented by Gassend et al. [29]. They suggested to equip each device $\mathcal{D}$ with a PUF that is used to frequently derive new device identifiers. Since verifiers cannot recompute these identifiers, they have access to a database that stores a tuple $(ID_1, ID_2, \ldots, ID_n)$ for each device, where $ID_i = \mathsf{PUF}(ID_{i-1})$ for $1 \leq i \leq n$ and ID_0 is a random device identifier. To authenticate to a verifier, $\mathcal{D}$ first sends its current identifier ID_j and then updates its identity to $ID_{j+1} = \mathsf{PUF}(ID_j)$. The verifier then checks whether there is a tuple that contains ID_j in the database. In the case where the verifier finds ID_j, it accepts $\mathcal{D}$ and invalidates all previous database entries ID_k with $k \leq j$ to prevent replay attacks. A limitation of this scheme is that $\mathcal{D}$ can be authenticated only n times without being re-initialized, which, as the authors mention, allows the adversary to perform denial-of-service attacks.

An alternative approach is using the PUF to generate the authentication secret of the device for use in a classical authentication protocol. The concept of PUF-based key storage has been presented by Gassend [28] and later generalized by Bringer et al. [16]. Instead of storing a cryptographic key in non-volatile memory, which is vulnerable to invasive hardware attacks, the idea is to extract the key from the physical properties of the PUF each time it is used. This should protect the key against unauthorized readout by invasive hardware attacks, such as probing attacks against non-volatile memory. Moreover, in the case where a tamper-evident PUF is used, any attempt to physically extract the key from the PUF circuit is assumed to change the challenge/response behavior of the PUF and to securely delete the key bound to the PUF. Since PUF responses are typically not uniformly random and affected by the varying operating conditions of the PUF, they cannot be used directly as cryptographic keys. Hence, privacy amplification, which adds additional entropy to the PUF response, and error correction techniques must be applied before a PUF response can be used as cryptographic key. The most common approach to achieve this are fuzzy extractors (cf. Section 2.3).

Tuyls et al. [122] proposed to use PUF-based key storage for the authentication secrets of RFID tags. Since the secrets are inherently hidden within the physical structure of the PUF, obtaining them by hardware-related attacks is supposed to be intractable for real-world adversaries [30]. Several other authentication schemes for embedded devices exist that use PUF-based key storage to protect against unauthorized tracking of devices [15, 99] and relay attacks [48].

6.1.2 PROTOCOL DESCRIPTION AND SPECIFICATION

The entities involved in the PUF-based authentication scheme are a device issuer $\mathcal{I}$, a verifier $\mathcal{V}$ (e.g., an RFID reader), and a device $\mathcal{D}$ (e.g., an RFID tag). The adversary is denoted with $\mathcal{A}$. The scheme enables *mutual authentication* between $\mathcal{V}$ and $\mathcal{D}$. $\mathcal{V}$ has access to a database DB containing CRPs of all devices $\mathcal{D}$ in the system. DB is initialized and maintained by $\mathcal{I}$.

Trust Model and Assumptions
Issuer $\mathcal{I}$ and verifier $\mathcal{V}$ are trusted, which is a typical assumption in most lightweight authentication systems. Further, $\mathcal{I}$ initializes $\mathcal{D}$ and $\mathcal{V}$ in a secure environment.

Device $\mathcal{D}$ is a passive device (e.g., an RFID tag) which cannot initiate communication, has a narrow communication range (a few centimeters to meters), and erases its temporary state (all session-specific information and randomness) after it gets out of the communication range of $\mathcal{V}$. Further, $\mathcal{D}$ is assumed to be equipped with a robust and unpredictable PUF (cf. Section 2.1), a reverse fuzzy extractor (cf. Section 2.3), and a cryptographic hash function.

Adversary $\mathcal{A}$ controls the wireless communication channel between $\mathcal{V}$ and $\mathcal{D}$. This means that $\mathcal{A}$ can eavesdrop, manipulate, delete, and reroute all protocol messages sent by $\mathcal{V}$ and $\mathcal{D}$. Moreover, $\mathcal{A}$ can obtain useful information (e.g., by visual observation) on whether $\mathcal{V}$ accepted $\mathcal{D}$ as a legitimate device. Following the typical assumptions on PUF-based key storage [62, 122, 131], $\mathcal{A}$ can read any information that is stored in the non-volatile memory of $\mathcal{D}$. However, $\mathcal{A}$ cannot access the responses of the PUF of $\mathcal{D}$ and cannot obtain temporary data stored in the volatile memory (such as intermediate results of the computations) of $\mathcal{D}$ while it is participating in an authentication protocol. This can be achieved by using side-channel aware designs for the implementation of the underlying algorithms.

Protocol Specification

System initialization   Issuer $\mathcal{I}$ stores a random device identifier ID in the non-volatile memory of device $\mathcal{D}$. Moreover, $\mathcal{I}$ extracts $q > 0$ CRPs $(x_1, y_1'), \ldots, (x_q, y_q')$ from the PUF of $\mathcal{D}$ and stores them together with ID in database DB, which is later used by verifier $\mathcal{V}$ in the authentication protocol.

Authentication protocol   The authentication protocol is depicted in Figure 6.1 and works as follows: verifier $\mathcal{V}$ starts by sending an authentication request $\texttt{auth}$ to device $\mathcal{D}$, which responds with its identifier ID. $\mathcal{V}$ uniformly samples a nonce N from the set of bit strings of length ℓ_N and a random CRP (x_i, y_i') from database DB and sends (x_i, N) to $\mathcal{D}$. Then, $\mathcal{D}$ evaluates $y_i \leftarrow \mathsf{PUF}(x_i)$, generates $h_i \leftarrow \mathsf{FEGen}(y_i)$ using the reverse fuzzy extractor (cf. Section 2.3), computes $a \leftarrow \mathsf{Hash}(ID, N, y_i, h_i)$, and sends (h_i, a) to $\mathcal{V}$. Next, $\mathcal{V}$ reproduces $y_i \leftarrow \mathsf{FERep}(y_i', h_i)$ using y_i' from DB and checks whether $\mathsf{Hash}(ID, N, y_i, h_i) = a$. If this is not the case, $\mathcal{V}$ aborts and rejects. Otherwise, $\mathcal{V}$ sends $b \leftarrow \mathsf{Hash}(a, y_i)$ to $\mathcal{D}$ and accepts. Eventually, $\mathcal{D}$ accepts if $\mathsf{Hash}(a, y_i) = b$ and rejects otherwise.

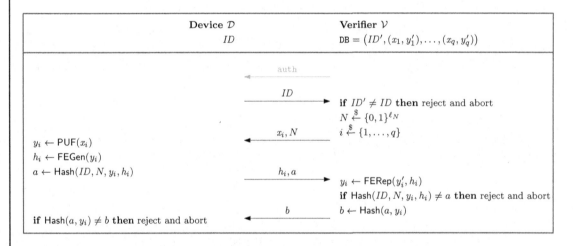

Figure 6.1: Lightweight PUF-based mutual authentication protocol.

Discussion   Note that the case where $q = 1$ is equivalent to PUF-based key storage, where y_1 represents the authentication secret of $\mathcal{D}$. In this case, x_1 can be stored in the non-volatile memory of $\mathcal{D}$ and needs not to be sent from $\mathcal{V}$ to $\mathcal{D}$. Hence, two protocol messages can be saved: N can be sent with $\texttt{auth}$ and ID can be sent with (h_i, a). Using multiple CRPs corresponds to storing multiple (session) keys in the PUF, which limits the impact of side channel attacks that may recover only a subset of these keys.

6.1.3 SECURITY ANALYSIS

In this section we informally discuss the security of the protocol in Section 6.1.2. A detailed security analysis can be found in the paper by van Herrewege et al. [38].

Security of reverse fuzzy extractors   Similar to conventional fuzzy extractors, reverse fuzzy extractors should ensure that the helper data does not leak the full PUF response. However, for reverse fuzzy extractors this must hold even when *multiple* different helper data for noisy variants of the *same* PUF response are known. This has been formalized by Boyen [13] as *outsider chosen perturbation security*. Further, Boyen showed [13] that certain fuzzy extractor constructions achieve outsider chosen perturbation security.

Correctness of the authentication protocol   Correctness means that, in the case where device $\mathcal{D}$ and verifier $\mathcal{V}$ are honest, mutual authentication should be successful. Van Herrewege et al. [38] showed that the mutual authentication scheme in Section 6.1.2 is correct when it is based on a secure sketch and a PUF that generates responses with a limited number of bit errors.

Device authentication   Device authentication means that adversary $\mathcal{A}$ should not be able to make a legitimate verifier $\mathcal{V}$ accept. This can be formalized based on a security experiment where $\mathcal{A}$ must make an honest $\mathcal{V}$ to authenticate $\mathcal{A}$ as an honest device $\mathcal{D}$ by arbitrarily interacting with $\mathcal{D}$ and $\mathcal{V}$. However, since in general it is not possible to prevent simple relay attacks, $\mathcal{A}$ is not allowed to just forward all messages from $\mathcal{D}$ to $\mathcal{V}$.[1] This means that at least some of the protocol messages that made $\mathcal{V}$ accept must have been computed by $\mathcal{A}$. Van Herrewege et al. [38] showed that the authentication scheme in Section 6.1.2 achieves device authentication in the random oracle model [8] (that models the hash function as a random function) when using a reverse fuzzy extractor that achieves outsider chosen perturbation security.

Verifier authentication   Verifier authentication means that adversary $\mathcal{A}$ should not be able to make an honest device $\mathcal{D}$ accept. This can be formalized by a verifier authentication security experiment which is identical to the device authentication experiment with the only difference that $\mathcal{A}$ wins, if $\mathcal{A}$ makes $\mathcal{D}$ accept after a limited number of queries. Van Herrewege et al. [38] showed that the authentication scheme in Section 6.1.2 achieves verifier authentication in the random oracle model [8] when using a reverse fuzzy extractor that achieves outsider chosen perturbation security and a PUF that generates at least a certain number of bit errors each time it is evaluated.

6.2 PUF-BASED ATTESTATION

Attestation is a mechanism to validate and to verify the integrity of a system's software state against malicious code. Various approaches to attestation have been proposed (see [85] for an overview).

---

[1]Note that simple relay attacks can be mitigated by distance bounding techniques [6, 14, 18, 36, 52, 86, 90, 110]. However, for simplicity we excluded relay attacks because the main focus of the protocol is demonstrating the use of reverse fuzzy extractors.

Common to all of them is that the platform to be evaluated (*prover*) sends a status report of its current configuration to another platform (*verifier*) to demonstrate that it is in a known and thus trustworthy state. Current attestation techniques can be viewed as a continuum ranging from fully hardware-supported attestation using secure coprocessors [78, 120] to attestation schemes requiring no explicit hardware support as in software-based attestation [27, 45, 56, 60, 105, 106]. The solutions based on security hardware modules (such as the TPM [120]) are inappropriate for resource-constrained embedded systems, while purely software-based attestation relies on strong assumptions, such as tamper-evident hardware and out-of-band (e.g., visual) prover authentication, which are hard to achieve in practice.

A practical lightweight attestation scheme for embedded devices should have low hardware overhead and reasonable attestation times. Software-based attestation follows this paradigm since it does not require any cryptographic secret or security hardware. However, software-based attestation cannot explicitly authenticate the underlying hardware components, making it vulnerable to impersonation attacks [103]. To address this problem timed attestation protocols have been proposed that bind the attestation algorithm to the underlying hardware, e.g., by exploiting the side-effects of processor operation [51] or by using security features in hardware [45, 56, 102]. However, these approaches have been shown to be ineffective [107] or they require secure hardware components that are again too complex or too expensive for resource-constrained embedded systems. In this context, PUFs are a promising primitive to bind the attestation protocol to a particular physical hardware platform and to enable lightweight remote attestation for embedded devices [55, 103].

In this section, we describe a PUF-based attestation scheme [55], which uses an ALU PUF (cf. Section 2.2.1) as hardware trust anchor. The tight-coupling of the ALU PUF with the processor architecture binds the attestation protocol to hardware characteristics, prevents impersonation attacks, thwarts hardware-based attacks, and requires only minimal hardware overhead since the ALU PUF reuses existing circuit structures of the processor.

6.2.1   PROTOCOL DESCRIPTION AND SPECIFICATION

In the attestation scheme, a *prover* P reports on the integrity of its (program) memory content S to a *verifier* V. While P is an embedded device with constrained resources (e.g., a sensor node), V is a more powerful computing device (e.g., a smartphone or a laptop). In the following, PUF() means a Controlled PUF (cf. Section 4.1) based on an ALU PUF, which includes an error correction mechanism (cf. Section 2.3).

Trust Model and Assumptions

As is common in the literature on timed attestation [27, 45, 56, 60, 105, 106], the attestation algorithm and its implementation used by P are assumed to be optimal in the sense that it is hard for adversary A to find another algorithm or implementation that can be executed by P in less time. Moreover, as in [103], the bandwidth of the communication interfaces of P is far lower

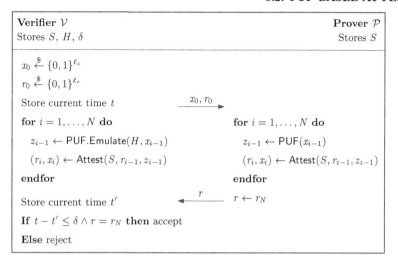

Figure 6.2: PUF-based attestation scheme.

than the bandwidth of the interface between the processor and the PUF of $\mathcal{P}$. Further, $\mathcal{V}$ can emulate the PUF of $\mathcal{P}$, e.g., using gate-level delay table H of the ALU PUF (cf. Section 4.2).

Adversary $\mathcal{A}$ can eavesdrop on and modify any data transmitted between $\mathcal{P}$ and $\mathcal{V}$. Further, $\mathcal{A}$ knows all data stored in the memory of $\mathcal{P}$ and can modify it. Note that by modifying the memory content of $\mathcal{P}$, $\mathcal{A}$ can change the program code and thus has full control of $\mathcal{P}$. However, $\mathcal{A}$ cannot clone PUF() of $\mathcal{P}$ and it is infeasible for $\mathcal{A}$ to predict output z of PUF() to a new challenge x for which $\mathcal{A}$ has never seen z before. Moreover, any attempt of $\mathcal{A}$ to modify the hardware of $\mathcal{P}$ to enhance its computing and/or memory capabilities changes the challenge/response behavior of PUF(). Finally, $\mathcal{V}$ is trusted.

Protocol Specification

The PUF-based attestation scheme works as follows (cf. Figure 6.2): verifier $\mathcal{V}$ chooses a PUF challenge $x_0 \overset{\$}{\leftarrow} \{0, 1\}^{\ell_x}$, which is a uniformly sampled bitstring of length ℓ_x, and an *attestation challenge* r_0, which is a uniformly sampled bitstring of length ℓ_r. Then $\mathcal{V}$ sends (x_0, r_0) to prover $\mathcal{P}$. Based on these challenges and its memory content S, $\mathcal{P}$ iteratively computes *attestation response r* using PUF() and attestation algorithm Attest(). After a certain number of iterations N, $\mathcal{P}$ sends r to $\mathcal{V}$, who accepts only if $\mathcal{P}$ responded within expected time bound δ and if r matches the expected attestation response. Hereby, $\mathcal{V}$ recomputes r using an emulation PUF.Emulate() of $\mathcal{P}$'s PUF().[2]

---

[2]Note that $\mathcal{V}$ can pre-compute the expected attestation response at any point in time before the attestation protocol-run with $\mathcal{P}$ or while it is waiting for $\mathcal{P}$'s response (as shown in Figure 6.2).

Instantiation

Attestation algorithm **Attest**() can be instantiated based on any known software-based attestation scheme (e.g., [20, 105, 136]) with only minor modifications to integrate the PUF [55, 103]. For instance, **Attest**() can be based on the algorithm in [105], which samples a memory word of S of prover $\mathcal{P}$ in each round and iteratively computes r [5]. This algorithm can be adapted to generate PUF challenges x_i and to take outputs z_i of **PUF**() as additional inputs in each round [55, 103].

6.2.2   SECURITY ANALYSIS

The attestation scheme should achieve *correctness* and *soundness* [5]. Correctness informally means that an honest $\mathcal{P}$, whose memory content matches the memory content S expected by $\mathcal{V}$, should always be accepted. Soundness informally means that it is infeasible for any $\mathcal{P}$ with a program memory content different from S to succeed in making $\mathcal{V}$ accept. Furthermore, the PUF-based attestation scheme should provide *prover authentication*, i.e., assure to $\mathcal{V}$ that the attestation algorithm has been computed by a particular $\mathcal{P}$.

In the following, we discuss the security of the PUF-based attestation scheme presented in Section 6.2.1. Note that, since **PUF**() is a Controlled PUF that includes an error correction mechanism, **PUF**() always returns the same output z to the same challenge x. Further, the underlying attestation scheme is assumed to be sound and correct.

Soundness   Due to the correctness of the underlying software-based attestation scheme and the robustness of **PUF**(), an honest prover $\mathcal{P}$ will always compute the correct attestation response r and be accepted by verifier $\mathcal{V}$.

Correctness   The PUF-based attestation scheme is based on a secure attestation scheme whose compression function has been modified to take the outputs z_i of **PUF**() as additional inputs using a similar approach as by Schulz et al. [103]. This minor modification preserves the structure of the attestation algorithm and does not affect the correctness property of the underlying software-based attestation scheme.

Prover authentication   The major objective of combining software-based attestation with PUFs is to assure to verifier $\mathcal{V}$ that attestation response r has been computed by prover $\mathcal{P}$ and not by any other device. There are two approaches for adversary $\mathcal{A}$ to violate prover authentication: (1) emulating **PUF**() of $\mathcal{P}$ on another device and (2) using **PUF**() of $\mathcal{P}$ as an oracle and computing r on another (potentially more powerful) device. By assumption, $\mathcal{A}$ does not know the gate-delay table H of **PUF**() and, since **PUF**() is a Controlled PUF, emulation attacks are infeasible in practice. Hence, it is infeasible for $\mathcal{A}$ to predict the correct outputs z_i of **PUF**() which are required to compute r. However, $\mathcal{A}$ could try to use **PUF**() of $\mathcal{P}$ as an oracle, meaning that whenever $\mathcal{A}$ needs an output z_i of **PUF**() for computing r, $\mathcal{A}$ may query **PUF**(). Since, by assumption, the bandwidth of the external communication interfaces of $\mathcal{P}$ is much lower than the bandwidth needed to transfer all z_i to $\mathcal{A}$ in time, $\mathcal{A}$ does not know at least one z_i. This means that $\mathcal{A}$ can predict the correct attestation response r only with the same probability as predicting the response of PUF(), which is very low.

Overclocking attack resiliency   One problem of the underlying attestation algorithm is that adversary $\mathcal{A}$ could simply overclock the processor of prover $\mathcal{P}$ to circumvent the enforcement of time-bound ι. The PUF-based attestation scheme resists this attack when based on an ALU PUF, which operates along with the processor clock network. Specifically, when $\mathcal{A}$ increases the clock frequency of the processor, the clock cycle time will be reduced. This impacts the setup time of the registers (flip-flop) used to store the raw PUF response (i.e., before error correction). Specifically, the clock edge may reach the output flip-flops of the ALU before the response is latched to them, resulting in wrong PUF responses.

CHAPTER 7

Security Model for PUF-based Systems

For the design and security analysis of cryptographic schemes based on Physically Unclonable Functions (PUFs) it is fundamental to have an appropriate formal security model. Currently, there is no widely accepted security model for PUFs while most PUF security models in the literature are not general enough since they exclude certain PUF types (as in [30, 84]), do not reflect the properties of real PUF implementations (as in [4, 30, 31, 84, 96]), or include security parameters that cannot be determined for PUF implementations in practice (as in [4, 17, 96]). Existing literature on PUF-based security schemes typically uses idealized PUF models that do *not* reflect *real* PUF implementations but the *desired* properties of *ideal* PUFs.

Exploiting physical properties in security systems raises important formalization problems. The core issues are to determine which properties of physical objects need to be defined and to find efficient ways to guarantee them in practice. In other words, one of the main challenges for using PUFs in future security applications is to properly integrate them into complex systems, where some of their physical properties can be a real advantage compared to purely algorithmic solutions. In this respect, useful and reasonable security definitions of PUFs should be both (1) sound for cryptographers in order to allow the analysis of PUF-based cryptographic systems, and (2) empirically verifiable, such that the security levels guaranteed by the physics can be evaluated (or at least be lower bounded).

7.1 LITERATURE OVERVIEW OF PUF SECURITY MODELS

One of the first approaches to formalize the security properties of PUFs was to model PUFs as *physical one-way functions* [91]. This definition does not cover most electronic PUFs since these are typically not one-way. A refined definition models PUFs as *physical random functions* [30], which does not cover PUFs with a small challenge/response space, such as memory-based PUFs. Another approach [31] formalizes PUFs as unclonable, unpredictable, and tamper-evident physical systems. In contrast to all previous PUF models, this is the first model that captures the fact that PUF responses are affected by varying operating conditions. This work distinguishes between *weak PUFs* and *strong PUFs*. Weak PUFs refer to PUFs with a small challenge/response space, such as memory-based PUFs, while strong PUFs mean PUFs with an exponential (in some security parameter) challenge/response space. Using the notion of weak and strong for the size of the challenge/response space can be misleading since in cryptography weak and strong are typically used to express the security level of a scheme. For example, the Arbiter PUF is a strong PUF but can be emulated very efficiently (cf. Section 3.1). Another PUF security model [96] presents two definitions: *physically obfuscated keys* for PUFs with a small challenge/response space size and a game-based security definition for PUFs with an exponential challenge/response space size. These definitions again do not capture varying operating conditions. A security model [4] proposed in the context of PUF-based encryption models PUFs as noisy, tamper-evident, and pseudo-random functions. Another PUF security model [17] defines PUFs as an ideal functionality in the universal composability (UC) framework [19]. This model is very complex and it is unclear how the underlying security parameters can be determined for PUF implementations.

7.2   FRAMEWORK FOR PHYSICAL FUNCTIONS

In this section, we give an overview of one of the most general security models for PUFs [3], which uses game-based security definitions to formalize the most important properties of PUFs for their integration into cryptographic protocols: robustness, unclonability, and unpredictability. This approach represents a modular and extensible security framework for physical functions in general and has been used to capture the properties of PUF implementations [3, 109] and in the design of PUF-based anti-counterfeiting mechanisms [108] and PUF-based cryptographic schemes [24].

7.2.1   BACKGROUND AND RATIONALE

This section explains the components and procedures relevant for deploying physical functions. Observe that the focus of the model discussed are not only PUFs but Physical Functions (PFs) in general where unclonability is only one possible security property. An overview of the security framework is given in Figure 7.1, which shows all components necessary for creating, evaluating, and post-processing the output of a PF. These components are explained in the following paragraphs.

Physical Function

A Physical Function (PF) consists of a *physical component* p that can be stimulated with some *challenge signal* $\tilde{x}$ which makes p respond with a corresponding *response signal* $\tilde{y}$. In addition to physical component p, a PF contains an *evaluation procedure* Eval that, on input a digital representation x of $\tilde{x}$, stimulates physical component p with $\tilde{x}$ and obtains the resulting response signal $\tilde{y}$. Finally, Eval returns a digital representation y of $\tilde{y}$. Note that with *procedure* we denote a probabilistic polynomial time algorithm that may involve some physical process such as the evaluation of a PUF. The challenge/response behavior of a PF heavily relies on the properties of physical component p, uncontrollable random noise (e.g., thermal noise and measurement uncertainties), and an evaluation parameter β_{PF} (e.g., a quantization factor) chosen by the PF manufacturer. Observe that the same physical component p can yield completely different PFs if combined with different evaluation procedures.

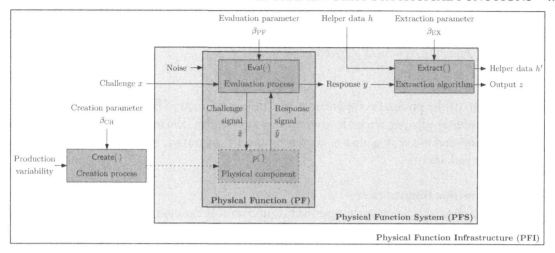

Figure 7.1: Generic framework for PFs.

Extraction Algorithm

Although the notion of a PF suggests differently, a PF is not a function in the classical sense. The main difference is that, when challenged with the same challenge x twice, a PF may produce different responses y. This is because the challenge/response behavior of a PF heavily relies on the physical properties of its physical component p, which is subject to uncontrollable random noise. The effects of noise can be removed up to a certain threshold by an *extraction algorithm* Extract (e.g., a fuzzy extractor [22, 23]; cf. Section 2.3), which maps slightly different responses y to the same challenge x to a unique output z according to some *extraction parameter* β_{EX}, which is typically chosen by the PF manufacturer or the PF user (i.e., the entity that integrates the PF into a higher-level protocol or algorithm). We assume that the extraction parameter specifies both the deployed extraction algorithm and all possible parameters (e.g., the number of output bits) of the Extract algorithm. The Extract algorithm can be executed in two different modes: *enrollment* and *reconstruction*. If challenge x is requested for the first time, enrollment mode is used to generate an output z and some *helper data* h'. Later, when challenge x is requested again together with helper data $h = h'$, reconstruction mode is used to recreate z. The purpose of helper data h' is to twofold [23]: (1) h' supports Extract in recreating the same output z for challenge x, and (2) h' allows binding given values (e.g., cryptographic keys) to a PF.

Physical Function System

As explained above, a PF is usually coupled with an appropriate extraction algorithm. Indeed, in a typical application scenario, a user will be aware only of the challenges given to the PF and the output returned by the extraction algorithm. Furthermore, for almost all relevant security notions, both the PF and the extraction algorithm determine whether a security property can be achieved or not. Therefore, it is a natural choice to abstract from Physical Function PF and extraction algorithm Extract and consider their combination as one single building block, which is denoted as Physical Function System (PF System).

Creation Process

The creation of the physical component p of a Physical Function PF is the result of a *creation process* Create, usually performed by the manufacturer of PF. The result of this process depends on a creation parameter β_{CR} that is chosen by the PF manufacturer and some uncontrollable production variability.

Physical Function Infrastructure

The combination of all previously described components is denoted with Physical Function Infrastructure (PF Infrastructure). Within a PF Infrastructure the creation, evaluation, and extraction parameters are *fixed*. Furthermore, these parameters uniquely specify the deployed procedures, e.g., β_{PF} defines the full details of the Eval procedure.

7.2.2   FORMALIZATION

The components and procedures within a PF Infrastructure as explained in Section 7.2.1 are formally defined in the following.

Definition 7.1   Physical Function (PF).   A *Physical Function* PF is a probabilistic procedure (i.e., a probabilistic polynomial time algorithm that may involve some physical process)

$$\mathsf{PF}_{p,\beta_{PF}} : X \to Y,$$

where X denotes the set of challenges and Y the set of responses. Internally, a PF is the combination of a physical component p and an evaluation procedure Eval which takes as input an extraction parameter β_{PF} and a challenge $x \in X$, i.e.,

$$y \leftarrow \mathsf{PF}_{p,\beta_{PF}}(x) = \mathsf{Eval}_p(\beta_{PF}, x).$$

Where appropriate, the specification of p and β_{PF} is discarded, that is PF is used instead of $\mathsf{PF}_{p,\beta_{PF}}$.

Definition 7.2   Physical Function System (PF System).   A *Physical Function System* PFS is a probabilistic procedure

$$\mathsf{PFS}_{p,\beta_{PF},\beta_{EX}} : X \times (H \cup \{\perp\}) \to Z \times H,$$

where X is the set of challenges, H the set of helper data values, $\perp$ the empty string, and Z the set of outputs. Internally, a PF System is the combination of a Physical Function $\mathsf{PF} = \mathsf{PF}_{p,\beta_{PF}}$ (Definition 7.1) and an extraction algorithm Extract, which is determined by an extraction parameter

β_{EX}:

$$(z, h') \leftarrow \mathsf{PFS}_{p,\beta_{\mathrm{PF}},\beta_{\mathrm{EX}}}(x, h) = \mathsf{Extract}_{\beta_{\mathrm{EX}}}\left(\mathsf{PF}_{p,\beta_{\mathrm{PF}}}(x), h\right).$$

Hereby, it is required that if $h \neq \bot$, then $h' = h$. Only in the case where $h = \bot$, a new helper data h' is generated for x. In the following, the internal components are omitted and the abbreviation $\mathsf{PFS} = \mathsf{PFS}_{p,\beta_{\mathrm{PF}},\beta_{\mathrm{EX}}}$ is used.

Note that $h = \bot$ means that $\mathsf{Extract}$ should be executed in enrollment mode and generate a new helper data h for challenge x. In the case where $h \neq \bot$, $\mathsf{Extract}$ should be executed in reconstruction mode and recreate output z associated with challenge x and helper data h. Note that, for the sake of consistent notation, in this case $h' = h$ is required to be returned by $\mathsf{Extract}$.

Definition 7.3 Creation Process. A creation process Create is a probabilistic procedure that, on input of a creation parameter β_{CR}, produces a physical component p (Definition 7.1), i.e., $p \leftarrow \mathsf{Create}(\beta_{\mathrm{CR}})$.

Definition 7.4 Physical Function Infrastructure (PF Infrastructure). A *Physical Function Infrastructure* $\mathcal{F}$ refers to a fixed creation process Create (Definition 7.3) and all PF Systems PFS (Definition 7.2) where the physical component p is the result of Create, i.e.,

$$\mathcal{F}_{\beta_{\mathrm{CR}}} = \left(\mathsf{Create}, \left\{\mathsf{PFS}_{p,\beta_{\mathrm{PF}},\beta_{\mathrm{EX}}} : p \leftarrow \mathsf{Create}(\beta_{\mathrm{CR}})\right\}\right),$$

where β_{CR}, β_{PF}, and β_{EX} are fixed.

7.3 ROBUSTNESS

7.3.1 RATIONALE

As explained in Section 7.2, a Physical Function (PF) might respond to the same challenge with different responses when queried several times. However, if these responses are "similar," it is possible to overcome this problem by using an appropriate extraction algorithm. Robustness refers to the property that former outputs of a PF System can be reconstructed at a later time. Obviously, a certain level of robustness is a necessary prerequisite for using PF Systems as functions in the classical sense.

Robustness could refer to at least two properties: (1) the ability to reconstruct the output of a PF System that has been produced by $\mathsf{Extract}$ in enrollment mode or (2) the ability to always recreate the same output in reconstruction mode (which may be different from the output in enrollment mode). The first option seems to be more appropriate for two reasons: first, one can show that a high probability for (1) implies a high probability for (2); and second, (1) reflects the basic requirement of a typical PUF-based key storage scenario.

7.3.2   FORMALIZATION

Following the consideration mentioned above, the robustness of a PF System is defined as follows.

Definition 7.5   Robustness.   Let PFS be a PF System (Definition 7.2) and let $x \in X$ be a challenge. The *challenge robustness* of PFS w.r.t. x is defined as the probability

$$\rho_{\mathsf{PFS}}(x) := \Pr\left[z' = z | (z, h) \leftarrow \mathsf{PFS}(x, \perp) \wedge (z', h') \leftarrow \mathsf{PFS}(x, h)\right].$$

This means that robustness is the probability that an output generated by Extract in reconstruction mode matches the output generated by Extract in enrollment mode.

7.4   PHYSICAL UNCLONABILITY

7.4.1   RATIONALE

In this section, the notion of *physical* unclonability is formally defined. Note that only clones on the physical level are considered while mathematical cloning attacks (as discussed in Section 3.1) are excluded. This restriction is motivated by the fact that an adversary in general has different possibilities for creating (i.e., cloning) a PF System that shows the "same" behavior as another PF System. For instance, the adversary could choose an Extract algorithm that maps all inputs to the same output. Clearly, two different PF Systems instances using this Extract algorithm would behave exactly the same, independent of the underlying PFs. It is obvious that protection against such attacks can be provided only by mechanisms outside the PF System. In general, while physical unclonability is an intrinsic feature, this is not true for mathematical unclonability, which hence is outside of the scope of a security model for PFs.

The following definition of physical unclonability can informally be stated as follows: *a PF System* PFS′ *is a physical clone of another PF System* PFS *if both PF Systems show the same behavior and deploy the same* Extract *algorithm.* The second condition guarantees that clonability is considered on a physical level only. It remains to discuss how to formalize the notion of "same behavior." Recall that PFs are assumed to be noisy in general, which raises the question of when two PF Systems can be considered being the same. A good starting point is to consider at first only one PF System. Recall that the extraction procedure is deployed to make a PF System "as deterministic as possible." Nonetheless, in certain cases, the same PF System might produce the same output twice only with a certain probability. This probability has been defined as the robustness of the PF System and termed $\rho_{\mathsf{PFS}}(x)$ in dependence of the considered challenge x (cf. Definition 7.5). Intuitively, a clone PFS′ cannot be more similar to the corresponding original PF System PFS than PFS itself. On the other hand, any PF System should be formally seen as a clone of itself. Therefore, robustness marks a natural upper bound on "how similar a clone can become" and it seems to be natural to integrate the notion of robustness into the definition of clones.

Another aspect that needs to be considered is the following: depending on the use case, only the responses of PFS to a subset of challenges might be known at all. Thus, any other PF

System PFS' that coincides on this subset of challenges could be seen as a clone. Therefore, it is sufficient that the definition of a clone captures only the set of challenges $X' \subseteq X$ that are relevant with regard to the underlying use case. Further, a cloning attack can have different meanings.

- *Selective cloning* refers to the event that for a *given* PF System PFS a clone PFS' is constructed.

- *Existential cloning* means that two arbitrary PF Systems PFS and PFS' are produced, where one is the clone of the other.

The difference between selective and existential cloning is that in the latter case no "original" PF System is given and instead, the adversary is free to choose which PF System he clones. Observe that this classification has some similarities to the security properties established for digital signatures and message authentication codes (MACs).

7.4.2   FORMALIZATION

A clone is defined as follows.

Definition 7.6   Physical Clone.   Let β_{PF} and β_{EX} be a fixed evaluation and extraction parameter, respectively. Moreover, let $\mathsf{PFS} = \mathsf{PFS}_{p,\beta_{\mathrm{PF}},\beta_{\mathrm{EX}}}$ and $\mathsf{PFS}' = \mathsf{PFS}_{p',\beta_{\mathrm{PF}},\beta_{\mathrm{EX}}}$ be two PF Systems (Definition 7.2) that are identical except of their physical component, i.e., $p \neq p'$. PFS' is a δ-*clone* of PFS with regard to $X' \subseteq X$ if for all $x \in X'$ it holds that:

$$\Pr\left[z' = z | (z, h) \leftarrow \mathsf{PFS}(x, \bot) \wedge (z', h') \leftarrow \mathsf{PFS}'(x, h)\right] \geq \delta \cdot \rho_{\mathsf{PFS}}(x).$$

For brevity, we write $\mathsf{PFS}' \stackrel{\delta, X'}{\equiv} \mathsf{PFS}$ if this equation holds.

Next, both notions of unclonability are formalized by means of two security experiments that specify the capabilities and the goal of adversary $\mathcal{A}$. On a high level, $\mathcal{A}$ is capable of creating arbitrary physical components, which in turn determine PF Systems. In practice, $\mathcal{A}$ will be limited to a certain set of creation processes, e.g., by increasing the sensitivity of his production facility. This is formally captured by allowing $\mathcal{A}$ to choose the creation parameter β_{CR} from a set B_{CR} of possible creation parameters. In practice, B_{CR} is expected to be small.

Existential Unclonability
Existential unclonability is defined as follows. In this scenario, which is depicted in Figure 7.2, $\mathcal{A}$ must produce two *arbitrary* clones and can query the **Create** process for $\beta_{\mathrm{CR}} \in B_{\mathrm{CR}}$ to create physical components p (cf. Definition 7.3). Note that a PF p implicitly defines a PF System $\mathsf{PFS} = \mathsf{PFS}_{p,\beta_{\mathrm{PF}},\beta_{\mathrm{EX}}}$ for some fixed evaluation and extraction parameter β_{PF} and β_{CR}, respectively (cf. Definition 7.2). Typically, only adversaries for which the time and computational effort

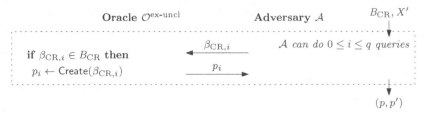

Figure 7.2: Existential unclonability security experiment $\mathbf{Exp}_{\mathcal{A}}^{\text{ex-uncl}}(q)$.

are bounded are relevant for practice. Hence, $\mathcal{A}$ is assumed to be able to do at most $q \geq 2$ queries to **Create**.

Definition 7.7 Existential Physical Unclonability. Let B_{CR} be a set of creation parameters and let β_{PF} and β_{EX} be fixed parameters for the evaluation and extraction procedures, respectively. Note that this implicitly defines a family $\mathcal{F}_{B_{\text{CR}}} := \{\mathcal{F}_{\beta_{\text{CR}}} : \beta_{\text{CR}} \in B_{\text{CR}}\}$ of PF Infrastructures (Definition 7.4). $\mathcal{F}_{B_{\text{CR}}}$ is called (γ, δ, q)-*existential-cloning-resistant* with regard to $X' \subseteq X$, if

$$\Pr\left[\text{PFS}'_{p',\beta_{\text{PF}},\beta_{\text{EX}}} \stackrel{\delta, X'}{\equiv} \text{PFS}_{p,\beta_{\text{PF}},\beta_{\text{EX}}} | (p, p') \leftarrow \mathbf{Exp}_{\mathcal{A}}^{\text{ex-uncl}}(q) \right.$$
$$\wedge\ p \in [\text{Create}(\beta_{\text{CR}})] \wedge \beta_{\text{CR}} \in B_{\text{CR}}$$
$$\left.\wedge\ p' \in [\text{Create}(\beta'_{\text{CR}})] \wedge \beta'_{\text{CR}} \in B_{\text{CR}}\right] \leq \gamma.$$

This means that the probability that $\mathcal{A}$ generated, as output of the security experiment depicted in Figure 7.2, two physical components p and p' which are clones on the PF System level and that have been created using the creation parameters $\beta_{\text{CR}} \in B_{\text{CR}}$, is less than γ. Note that Definition 7.7 covers different situations.

- *Honest manufacturer:* This case reflects the probability that an honest manufacturer creates two clones by coincidence and captures clonable PFs. In the case of $B_{\text{CR}} = \{\beta_{\text{CR}}\}$, i.e., where only one creation parameter is involved, the set $\mathcal{F}_{B_{\text{CR}}}$ "collapses" to a single PF Infrastructure $\mathcal{F}_{\beta_{\text{CR}}}$. Likewise, $\mathcal{A}$ can perform **Create** only with this specific creation parameter. In other words, $\mathcal{A}$ is restricted to actions that an honest manufacturer could do within $\mathcal{F}_{\beta_{\text{CR}}}$.

- *Malicious manufacturer:* This case covers the scenario, where B_{CR} contains more than one possible choice for the creation parameter β_{CR}, which allows $\mathcal{A}$ to influence the **Create** process in order to create a clone.

Selective Unclonability

Selective physical unclonability is defined in terms of the security experiment depicted in Figure 7.3. The difference to the security experiment of existential unclonability is that $\mathcal{A}$ is *given* a

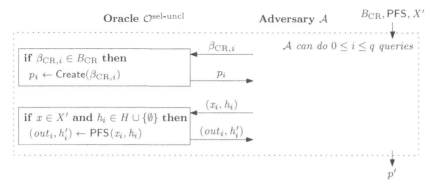

Figure 7.3: Selective unclonability security experiment $\mathbf{Exp}_{\mathcal{A}}^{\text{sel-uncl}}(q)$.

PF System PFS for which $\mathcal{A}$ must create a clone. Therefore, in addition to queries to Create, $\mathcal{A}$ is allowed to query PFS with challenges $x \in X'$. Again, only restricted adversaries $\mathcal{A}$ that can do at most $q \geq 1$ queries to Create and PFS are considered.

Definition 7.8 Selective Physical Unclonability. Let B_{CR} be a set of creation parameters and let β_{PF} and β_{EX} be fixed parameters for the evaluation and extraction procedures, respectively. Moreover, let $\mathcal{F}_{B_{\text{CR}}} := \{\mathcal{F}_{\beta_{\text{CR}}} : \beta_{\text{CR}} \in B_{\text{CR}}\}$ be the corresponding set of PF Infrastructures (Definition 7.4). Further, let PFS be a PF system (Definition 7.2) within the family of PF Infrastructures $\mathcal{F}_{B_{\text{CR}}}$, i.e., PFS $\in \{$PFS : PFS $\leftarrow$ Create$(\beta_{\text{CR}}) \wedge \beta_{\text{CR}} \in B_{\text{CR}}\}$. The adversary is denoted with $\mathcal{A}$. PFS is called (γ, δ, q)-*selective-cloning-resistant* w.r.t. $X' \in X$, if

$$\Pr\left[\text{PFS}'_{p',\beta_{\text{PF}},\beta_{\text{EX}}} \stackrel{\delta,X'}{\equiv} \text{PFS}_{p,\beta_{\text{PF}},\beta_{\text{EX}}} \,\middle|\, p' \leftarrow \mathbf{Exp}_{\mathcal{A}}^{\text{ex-uncl}}(q) \right.$$
$$\left. \wedge\ p' \in [\text{Create}(\beta_{\text{CR}})] \wedge \beta_{\text{CR}} \in B_{\text{CR}}\right] \leq \gamma.$$

7.5 UNPREDICTABILITY

7.5.1 RATIONALE

One common application of PUFs is to use them to securely generate secret values (e.g., cryptographic keys). Examples include secure key storage [62, 122, 131] and hardware-entangled cryptography [4]. Such applications implicitly require that the adversary cannot predict the output of a PF System. Moreover, for typical PUF-based challenge/response identification protocols (cf. Section 6.1) it is important that the adversary cannot predict the response to a new challenge from previously observed challenge/response pairs (CRPs). Therefore, the notion of *unpredictability* is an important property that needs to be included into a model for PFs.

Classically, the notion of unpredictability of a random function f is formalized by the following security experiment consisting of a *learning* and a *challenge* phase. In the learning phase, $\mathcal{A}$ learns the evaluations of f on a set of inputs $\{x_1, \ldots, x_n\}$ which may be given from outside or chosen by $\mathcal{A}$. Then, in the challenge phase, $\mathcal{A}$ must return $(x, f(x))$ for some $x \notin \{x_1, \ldots, x_n\}$. Given that this formalization is common and widely accepted in cryptography, one may be tempted to adapt it in a straightforward manner to PUFs. This would mean to take the same definition but to consider PF Systems instead of functions. However, this approach does not always make sense. First, the output of a PF System depends on a challenge x *and* some helper data h. Thus, h must be taken into account. Moreover, different applications may require different variants of unpredictability. For instance, the concept of PUF-based key storage is to use a PF System for securely storing a cryptographic secret k. This secret k is usually derived from the output z of a PF System for some input x. In some cases, x is public and/or possibly fixed for all instantiations. Note that in such a scenario it is required that each device generates a different secret k for the same challenge x. Hence, the outputs of different devices (i.e., their PF Systems) should be independent. This requirement is captured by the following security experiment. Given the outputs $\mathsf{PFS}_1(x, \bot), \ldots, \mathsf{PFS}_n(x, \bot)$ of n different PF Systems instances to challenge x in the learning phase, adversary $\mathcal{A}$ has to predict output $\mathsf{PFS}(x, \bot)$ for another PF System $\mathsf{PFS} \notin \{\mathsf{PFS}_1, \ldots, \mathsf{PFS}_n\}$ in the challenge phase. Clearly, there is a fundamental difference between the classical definition of unpredictability and this security experiment: in the original definition of unpredictability, $\mathcal{A}$ is given the evaluation of *one* PF System on *many* challenges, while in the latter experiment $\mathcal{A}$ learns the evaluation of *many* PF Systems on *one* single challenge.

Obviously, a useful definition of unpredictability of a PF System should cover both unpredictability in the original sense *and* independence of the outputs of different PF Systems instances. Therefore, we define a security experiment that involves the following sets: let P_L be the set of PF Systems that are allowed to be queried by $\mathcal{A}$ in the learning phase; let P_C be the set of PF Systems that are allowed to be queried by $\mathcal{A}$ in the challenge phase; and let X be the set of challenges that are allowed to be queried by $\mathcal{A}$ during the whole experiment. Consider the following two extreme cases.[1]

1. *Independence of the outputs of a single PF System:* Consider the case where $P_L = P_C = \{\mathsf{PFS}\}$ consists of one single PF System only, while X contains several challenges. During the learning phase, adversary $\mathcal{A}$ learns $\mathsf{PFS}(x_i)$ for several challenges $x_i \in X$. Later, in the challenge phase, $\mathcal{A}$ has to predict $\mathsf{PFS}(x)$ for a new challenge $x \in X$. It is easy to see that this is the direct translation of the classical unpredictability experiment described at the beginning of this section to the scenario of physical function systems.

2. *Independence of the outputs of different PF Systems instances:* Now consider the scenario, where $X = \{x\}$ consists of one single challenge only, while P_L and P_C contain several PF Systems. In this case, during the learning phase, $\mathcal{A}$ learns $\mathsf{PFS}_i(x)$ for several different PF Systems

---

[1]For the sake of readability the helper data is omitted here.

instances $PFS_i \in P_L$. Afterwards, in the challenge phase, $\mathcal{A}$ has to predict $PFS(x)$ for a *new* PF System $PFS \in P_C$ that has not been queried before. This reflects the requirements of PUF-based key storage.

The definition of unpredictability should cover both extreme and all intermediate cases.

7.5.2 FORMALIZATION

Armknecht et al. [3] defined to notions of unpredictability: *weak unpredictability* and *strong unpredictability*. Weak unpredictability corresponds to a passive adversary who does not interact with PF Systems but only observes their outputs. In contrast, strong unpredictability covers active adversaries who may adaptively query different PF Systems instances. The consideration of weak unpredictability is important for at least the following reasons: (1) weak unpredictability is an established property in cryptography and has been used for stronger cryptographic constructions [87], and (2) PF constructions may be weakly unpredictable only, e.g., Arbiter PUFs (cf. Section 5.3.2), and should be covered by the model.

Weak Unpredictability

The definition of weak unpredictability is based on the security experiment $\mathbf{Exp}_{\mathcal{A}}^{\text{w-uprd}}$ shown in Figure 7.4, which is played between adversary $\mathcal{A}$ and oracle $\mathcal{O}^{\text{w-upred}}$. The experiment consists of a learning phase and a challenge phase. In the learning phase, $\mathcal{A}$ learns the outputs z_i and helper data h_i of different PF Systems instances PFS_i to a set of given challenges x_i. In the challenge phase, $\mathcal{A}$ must predict the output z of a PF System PFS to a new challenge x and helper data h which have not been used in the learning phase.

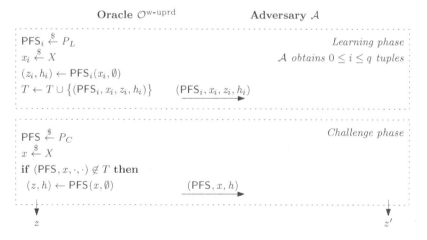

Figure 7.4: Weak unpredictability security experiment $\mathbf{Exp}_{\mathcal{A}}^{\text{w-uprd}}(q)$.

Definition 7.9   Weak Unpredictability.   Let $P_L, P_C \subseteq P$ be subsets of the set of all possible PF Systems P. Let $T = \{\}$ and $q \in \mathbb{N}$ with $q \geq 0$. The adversary is denoted with $\mathcal{A}$ and takes part in the security experiment depicted in Figure 7.4. A PF System is *weak* (λ, q)*-unpredictable* if

$$\Pr\left[z = z' | (z, z') \leftarrow \mathbf{Exp}_{\mathcal{A}}^{\text{w-uprd}}(q)\right] \leq \lambda \cdot \rho_{\mathsf{PFS}}(x).$$

Note that the robustness of a PF System is an upper bound of the predictability of its outputs. For instance, a true random number generator is a PF System with very high unpredictability but low reliability.

Strong Unpredictability

Some use cases require a stronger notion of unpredictability where the adversary is allowed to adaptively query the PF System in the challenge phase. Therefore, strong unpredictability is defined based on security experiment $\mathbf{Exp}_{\mathcal{A}}^{\text{s-uprd}}$, which is depicted in Figure 7.5. The security experiment is similar to the experiment of weak unpredictability but adversary $\mathcal{A}$ can adaptively interact with the PF Systems. Specifically, in the learning phase, $\mathcal{A}$ can adaptively query any PF System PFS_i for challenge x_i and helper data h_i, and obtain the corresponding output z_i. Further, in the challenge phase, $\mathcal{A}$ can choose PF System PFS, challenge x, and helper data h for which $\mathcal{A}$ must predict output z.

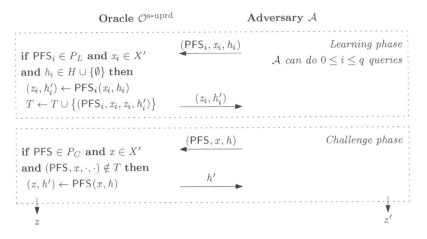

Figure 7.5: Strong unpredictability security experiment $\mathbf{Exp}_{\mathcal{A}}^{\text{s-uprd}}(q)$.

Definition 7.10   Strong Unpredictability.   Let P_L be the set of PF Systems that are allowed to be queried by $\mathcal{A}$ in the learning phase and let P_C be the set of PF Systems that are allowed to be queried by $\mathcal{A}$ in the challenge phase. Moreover, let $T = \{\}$ and $q \in \mathbb{N}$ with $q \geq 0$. The adversary is denoted with $\mathcal{A}$ and takes part in the security experiment depicted in Figure 7.5. A PF System is *strong* (λ, q)*-unpredictable* if

$$\Pr\left[z = z' | (z, z') \leftarrow \mathbf{Exp}_{\mathcal{A}}^{\text{s-uprd}}(q)\right] \leq \lambda \cdot \rho_{\mathsf{PFS}}(x).$$

7.6 CONCLUSION

The PUF security model presented in this chapter focuses on the minimum requirements on PUF and has been used to estimate the robustness and unclonability properties of different PUFs types [3, 109] as well as in the context of designing anti-counterfeiting mechanisms [108] and physical hash functions [24].

One of the important remaining challenges is the extension of this framework to definitions of other security-relevant properties of PUFs, e.g., tamper-evidence, meaning the property that unauthorized manipulations of PUFs are detectable. Another challenge is to develop new cryptographic mechanisms based on PUFs where the security can be reduced to the (alleged) properties of the deployed PUFs.

CHAPTER 8

Conclusion

Since the introduction of Physically Unclonable Functions (PUFs), researchers proposed many different PUF designs and a large variety of PUF-based security mechanisms. PUFs were first celebrated as promising cryptographic primitives. Over the years many researchers investigated various aspects of PUFs including their design, implementation, and protocol integration as well as attacks on PUFs and PUF-based systems.

In this book, we gave an overview of PUFs, their design, the underlying assumptions, and the properties of their implementations. We discussed how PUFs can be integrated into cryptographic protocols on the example of PUF-based device authentication and PUF-based remote attestation. Further, we gave a flavor of the formal modeling of PUFs and PUF-based cryptographic schemes, which is essential for the security analysis of PUF-based systems and still in its beginning.

Recent research shows that further investigations are necessary (see, e.g., [97]), particularly with regard to the design and implementation of novel and practical PUF concepts that are secure against emulation attacks and the security analysis of PUF implementations, as discussed in the following.

Practical PUF designs   Many known electronic PUFs can be compromised: memory-based PUFs can be read out completely since they have only a limited response space and most delay-based PUFs can be emulated using machine learning techniques (cf. Section 3.1). While these PUFs can still be used in many applications, such as PUF-based key storage [62, 122, 131] and Controlled PUFs (cf. Section 4.1) where the adversary cannot access the challenge/response pairs of the PUF, the use of these PUFs in applications with strong unclonability and unpredictability requirements, such as cryptographic protocols (cf. Chapter 6), must be carefully considered. Furthermore, PUF responses can be verified only when the verifier has access to a database of previously recorded challenge/response pairs (CRPs), which may lead to scalability problems in practice. Hence, one open challenge is the design and implementation of novel PUF concepts that achieve the requirements of existing theoretical PUF-based security solutions in the literature, including resistance to emulation attacks, large challenge/response spaces to prevent complete readout of the PUF, public verifiability (i.e., no CRP database required to verify PUF responses), tamper-evidence, physical reconfigurability, and a small hardware footprint. Another challenge in this context is the secure integration of PUFs into embedded devices such that all algorithms and circuits storing and processing the PUF response are protected against physical attacks, including side-channel attacks and invasive attacks. Current works (e.g., [10]) in this area focus on the design of novel PUF concepts and their implementation to overcome these limitations.

Security analysis of PUF implementations   Many PUF-based applications, such as PUF-based key storage [62, 122, 131], require PUF responses to be inaccessible to the adversary, which is typically justified by the assumption that the PUF is tamper-evident. However, even when a tamper-evident PUF (such as a Coating PUF [88, 123, 129]; cf. Section 2.2.3) is used, it is currently unclear whether existing PUF implementations in integrated circuits (ICs) leak information on their response over side channels, such as electro-magnetic radiation, power consumption, or remanence decay effects. Hence, the analysis of the side-channel leakage of known PUF implementations and their resistance to invasive hardware attacks are important open research problems. Current research (e.g., [64]) in this area develops new models and refines existing ones to more accurately capture the physical and cryptographic properties of PUFs.

Terms and Abbreviations

AES (Advanced Encryption Standard)

A specification for the encryption of electronic data [76]. 24, 63

ALU (Arithmetic Logic Unit)

A digital circuit that performs integer arithmetic and logical operations. 8, 9, 42, 43, 45, 63

ASIC (Application-specific Integrated Circuit)

An integrated circuit (IC) customized for a particular use. 2, 5, 9, 10, 20, 23–30, 63

BER (Bit Error Rate)

Indicates the fraction of bits in a bitstring that are different from a reference bitstring. 25, 26, 30–32, 35, 63

CMOS (Complementary Metal-Oxide Semiconductor)

A technology for constructing ICs. 23, 63

CRP (Challenge/Response Pair)

A tuple of the digital representations of a PUF input signal (challenge) and the corresponding PUF output signal (response). 9, 16, 19, 20, 25, 26, 28, 37–40, 55, 61, 63

CTW (Contect-Tree Weighting)

A lossless compression algorithm [134]. 27, 63

FF (Flip-flop)

A circuit that has two stable states and can be used to store one bit of information. 2, 4, 8, 9, 11, 23–26, 30, 32, 35, 45, 63

FIB (Focussed Ion Beam)

A technology particularly used in the semiconductor industry and materials science for analysis, deposition, and ablation of materials. 17, 63

FPGA (Field-programmable Gate Array)

An integrated circuit (IC) designed to be configured by a customer or a designer after manufacturing. 5–7, 10, 11, 20, 25, 63

IC (Integrated Circuit)

A set of electronic circuits on a plate of semiconductor material. 3–5, 8, 12, 23, 62–64

LR-PUF (Logically Reconfigurable PUF)

An advanced PUF concept that allows changing the PUF challenge/response behavior after deployment of the PUF (cf. Section 4.3). 20, 21, 64

PF (Physical Function)

A physical object that generates a response signal when stimulated with a challenge signal (cf. Section 7.2.1). 48–55, 57, 64

PFI (Physical Function Infrastructure)

The combination of a Physical Function System (PF System) and an creation procedure (cf. Section 7.2.1). 50, 51, 54, 55

PFS (Physical Function System)

The combination of a Physical Function (PF) and an extractor algorithm (cf. Section 7.2.1). 50–59, 64

PUF (Physically Unclonable Function)

A noisy function embedded into a physical object, e.g., an integrated circuit (cf. Section 2.1). 1–17, 19–21, 23–35, 37–45, 47, 48, 51, 55–57, 59, 61–64

RFID (Radio-frequency Identification)

A wireless communication technology intended for the automatic identification of transceivers attached to objects. 3, 39, 64

SIMPL (Simulation Possible but Laborious)

An advanced PUF concept that allows verifying responses based on an emulation of the PUF (cf. Section 4.2). 19, 20, 64

SRAM (Static Random-Access Memory)

Volatile semiconductor memory technology. 4, 9–11, 17, 23, 24, 26, 29, 30, 32, 35, 38, 64

TPM (Trusted Platform Module)

A specification [120] for a cryptographic processor included with some personal computers. 42, 64

TSMC (Taiwan Semiconductor Manufacturing Company, Ltd.)

A semiconductor foundry. 24, 64

Bibliography

[1] K. D. Akdemir, Z. Wang, M. G. Karpovsky, and B. Sunar. Design of cryptographic devices resilient to fault injection attacks using nonlinear robust codes. *Fault Analysis in Cryptography*, 2011. DOI: 10.1007/978-3-642-29656-7_11. 21

[2] Ittai Anati, Shay Gueron, Simon P. Johnson, and Vincent R. Scarlata. Innovative technology for CPU based attestation and sealing. In *Workshop on Hardware and Architectural Support for Security and Privacy (HASP)*. ACM, 2013. 1

[3] Frederik Armknecht, Roel Maes, Ahmad-Reza Sadeghi, François-Xavier Standaert, and Christian Wachsmann. A formal foundation for the security features of physical functions. In *IEEE Symposium on Security and Privacy (S&P)*, pages 397–412. IEEE, Washington, DC, USA, May 2011. DOI: 10.1109/SP.2011.10. 1, 3, 12, 25, 26, 27, 29, 48, 57, 59

[4] Frederik Armknecht, Roel Maes, Ahmad-Reza Sadeghi, Berk Sunar, and Pim Tuyls. Memory leakage-resilient encryption based on physically unclonable functions. In *Advances in Cryptology (ASIACRYPT)*, volume 5912 of *Lecture Notes in Computer Science (LNCS)*, pages 685–702. Springer, Berlin/Heidelberg, Germany, December 2009. DOI: 10.1007/978-3-642-10366-7_40. 3, 12, 20, 47, 48, 55

[5] Frederik Armknecht, Ahmad-Reza Sadeghi, Steffen Schulz, and Christian Wachsmann. A security framework for the analysis and design of software attestation. In *ACM Conference on Computer and Communications Security (CCS)*, pages 1–12. ACM, New York, NY, USA, November 2013. DOI: 10.1145/2508859.2516650. 44

[6] Gildas Avoine and Aslan Tchamkerten. An efficient distance bounding RFID authentication protocol: Balancing false-acceptance rate and memory requirement. In *Information Security Conference (ISC)*, volume 5735 of *Lecture Notes in Computer Science (LNCS)*, pages 250–261. Springer, Berlin/Heidelberg, Germany, September 2009. DOI: 10.1007/978-3-642-04474-8_21. 41

[7] Nathan Beckmann and Miodrag Potkonjak. Hardware-based public-key cryptography with public physically unclonable functions. In *Information Hiding (IH)*, volume 5806 of *Lecture Notes in Computer Science (LNCS)*, pages 206–220. Springer, Berlin/Heidelberg, Germany, June 2009. DOI: 10.1007/978-3-642-04431-1_15. 19

[8] Mihir Bellare and Phillip Rogaway. Random oracles are practical: A paradigm for designing efficient protocols. In *ACM Conference on Computer and Communications*

Security (CCS), pages 62–73. ACM, New York, NY, USA, November 1993. DOI: 10.1145/168588.168596. 41

[9] Mudit Bhargava, Cagla Cakir, and Ken Mai. Comparison of bi-stable and delay-based physical unclonable functions from measurements in 65nm bulk CMOS. In *Custom Integrated Circuits Conference (CICC)*, pages 1–4. IEEE, Washington, DC, USA, September 2012. DOI: 10.1109/CICC.2012.6330625. 23

[10] Mudit Bhargava and Ken Mai. A high reliability PUF using hot carrier injection based response reinforcement. In *Cryptographic Hardware and Embedded Systems (CHES)*, volume 8086 of *Lecture Noted in Computer Science (LNCS)*, pages 90–106. Springer, Berlin/Heidelberg, Germany, 2013. DOI: 10.1007/978-3-642-40349-1_6. 62

[11] Leonid Bolotnyy and Gabriel Robins. Physically unclonable function-based security and privacy in RFID systems. In *Conference on Pervasive Computing and Communications (PerCom)*, pages 211–220. IEEE, Washington, DC, USA, March 2007. DOI: 10.1109/PERCOM.2007.26. 37, 38

[12] Christoph Bösch, Jorge Guajardo, Ahmad-Reza Sadeghi, Jamshid Shokrollahi, and Pim Tuyls. Efficient helper data key extractor on FPGAs. In *Cryptographic Hardware and Embedded Systems (CHES)*, volume 5154 of *Lecture Notes in Computer Science (LNCS)*, pages 181–197. Springer, Berlin/Heidelberg, Germany, July 2008. DOI: 10.1007/978-3-540-85053-3_12. 13, 37

[13] Xavier Boyen. Reusable cryptographic fuzzy extractors. In *ACM Conference on Computer and Communications Security (CCS)*, pages 82–91. ACM, New York, NY, USA, October 2004. DOI: 10.1145/1030083.1030096. 14, 16, 41

[14] Stefan Brands and David Chaum. Distance-Bounding protocols. In *Advances in Cryptology (EUROCRYPT)*, volume 765 of *Lecture Notes in Computer Science (LNCS)*, pages 344–359. Springer, Berlin/Heidelberg, Germany, May 1994. DOI: 10.1007/3-540-48285-7_30. 41

[15] Julien Bringer, Hervé Chabanne, and Thomas Icart. Improved privacy of the tree-based hash protocols using physically unclonable function. In *Security and Cryptography for Networks (SCN)*, volume 5229 of *Lecture Notes in Computer Science (LNCS)*, pages 77–91. Springer, Berlin/Heidelberg, Germany, August 2008. DOI: 10.1007/978-3-540-85855-3_6. 39

[16] Julien Bringer, Hervé Chabanne, and Thomas Icart. Efficient zero-knowledge identification schemes which respect privacy. In *ACM Symposium on Information, Computer and Communications Security (ASIACCS)*, pages 195–205. ACM, New York, NY, USA, March 2009. DOI: 10.1145/1533057.1533086. 20, 38

[17] Christina Brzuska, Marc Fischlin, Heike Schröder, and Stefan Katzenbeisser. Physically uncloneable functions in the universal composition framework. In *Advances in Cryptology (CRYPTO)*, volume 6841 of *Lecture Notes in Computer Science (LNCS)*, pages 51–70. Springer, Berlin/Heidelberg, Germany, August 2011. DOI: 10.1007/978-3-642-22792-9_4. 47, 48

[18] Laurent Bussard and Walid Bagga. Distance-Bounding proof of knowledge to avoid Real-Time attacks. In *Security and Privacy in the Age of Ubiquitous Computing*, volume 181, pages 223–238. Springer US, May 2005. DOI: 10.1007/0-387-25660-1_15. 41

[19] Ran Canetti. Universally composable security: A new paradigm for cryptographic protocols. In *IEEE Symposium on Foundations of Computer Science*, pages 136–145. IEEE, Washington, DC, USA, October 2001. DOI: 10.1109/SFCS.2001.959888. 48

[20] Young-Geun Choi, Jeonil Kang, and DaeHun Nyang. Proactive code verification protocol in wireless sensor network. In *Computational Science and Its Applications (ICCSA)*, volume 4706 of *Lecture Notes in Computer Science (LNCS)*, pages 1085–1096. Springer, Berlin/Heidelberg, Germany, 2007. DOI: 10.1007/978-3-540-74477-1_97. 44

[21] Srinivas Devadas, Edward Suh, Sid Paral, Richard Sowell, Tom Ziola, and Vivek Khandelwal. Design and implementation of PUF-based unclonable RFID ICs for anti-counterfeiting and security applications. In *IEEE International Conference on RFID*, pages 58–64. IEEE, Washington, DC, USA, April 2008. DOI: 10.1109/RFID.2008.4519377. 37, 38

[22] Yevgeniy Dodis, Jonathan Katz, Leonid Reyzin, and Adam Smith. Robust fuzzy extractors and authenticated key agreement from close secrets. In *Advances in Cryptology (CRYPTO)*, volume 4117 of *Lecture Notes in Computer Science (LNCS)*, pages 232–250. Springer, Berlin/Heidelberg, Germany, August 2006. DOI: 10.1109/TIT.2012.2200290. 12, 16, 49

[23] Yevgeniy Dodis, Leonid Reyzin, and Adam Smith. Fuzzy extractors: How to generate strong keys from biometrics and other noisy data. In *Advances in Cryptology (EUROCRYPT)*, volume 3027 of *Lecture Notes in Computer Science (LNCS)*, pages 523–540. Springer, Berlin/Heidelberg, Germany, May 2004. DOI: 10.1007/978-3-540-24676-3_31. 12, 13, 14, 37, 49

[24] François Durvaux, Benoît Gérard, Stéphanie Kerckhof, François Koeune, and François-Xavier Standaert. Intellectual property protection for integrated systems using soft physical hash functions. In *Information Security Applications*, volume 7690 of *Lecture Notes in Computer Science (LNCS)*, pages 208–225. Springer, August 2012. DOI: 10.1007/978-3-642-35416-8_15. 48, 59

[25] Ilze Eichhorn, Patrick Koeberl, and Vincent van der Leest. Logically reconfigurable PUFs: Memory-based secure key storage. In *ACM Workshop on Scalable Trusted Computing (STC)*, pages 59–64. ACM, New York, NY, USA, October 2011. DOI: 10.1145/2046582.2046594. 3

[26] Karim Eldefrawy, Aurelien Francillon, Daniele Perito, and Gene Tsudik. SMART: Secure and minimal architecture for (establishing a dynamic) root of trust. In *Network and Distributed System Security Symposium (NDSS)*, 2012. 1

[27] Ryan W. Gardner, Sujata Garera, and Aviel D. Rubin. Detecting code alteration by creating a temporary memory bottleneck. *Trans. Info. For. Sec.*, 4(4):638–650, 2009. DOI: 10.1109/TIFS.2009.2033231. 42

[28] Blaise Gassend. Physical random functions. Master's thesis, Department of Electrical Engineering and Computer Science, Massachusetts Institute of Technology (MIT), February 2003. 7, 20, 27, 38

[29] Blaise Gassend, Dwaine Clarke, Marten van Dijk, and Srinivas Devadas. Controlled physical random functions. In *Annual Computer Security Applications Conference (ACSAC)*, pages 149–160. IEEE, Washington, DC, USA, December 2002. DOI: 10.1109/CSAC.2002.1176287. 15, 38

[30] Blaise Gassend, Dwaine Clarke, Marten van Dijk, and Srinivas Devadas. Silicon physical random functions. In *ACM Conference on Computer and Communications Security (CCS)*, pages 148–160. ACM, New York, NY, USA, November 2002. DOI: 10.1145/586110.586132. 4, 7, 8, 19, 27, 39, 47

[31] Jorge Guajardo, Sandeep Kumar, Geert-Jan Schrijen, and Pim Tuyls. FPGA intrinsic PUFs and their use for IP protection. In *Cryptographic Hardware and Embedded Systems (CHES)*, volume 4727 of *Lecture Notes in Computer Science (LNCS)*, pages 63–80. Springer, Berlin/Heidelberg, Germany, September 2007. DOI: 10.1007/978-3-540-74735-2_5. 3, 4, 10, 27, 47

[32] Jorge Guajardo, Sandeep S. Kumar, Geert-Jan Schrijen, and Pim Tuyls. Physical unclonable functions and public-key crypto for FPGA IP protection. In *Field Programmable Logic and Applications (FPL)*, pages 189–195. IEEE, Washington, DC, USA, August 2007. DOI: 10.1109/FPL.2007.4380646. 10

[33] Jorge Guajardo, Sandeep S. Kumar, Geert-Jan Schrijen, and Pim Tuyls. Brand and IP protection with physical unclonable functions. In *IEEE International Symposium on Circuits and Systems (ISCAS)*, pages 3186–3189. IEEE, Washington, DC, USA, May 2008. DOI: 10.1109/ISCAS.2008.4542135. 3

[34] Ghaith Hammouri, Aykutlu Dana, and Berk Sunar. CDs have fingerprints too. In *Cryptographic Hardware and Embedded Systems (CHES)*, volume 5747 of *Lecture Notes in Computer Science (LNCS)*, pages 348–362. Springer, Berlin/Heidelberg, Germany, September 2009. DOI: 10.1007/978-3-642-04138-9_25. 23, 27

[35] Ghaith Hammouri, Erdinç Öztürk, Berk Birand, and Berk Sunar. Unclonable lightweight authentication scheme. In *International Conference on Information and Communications Security (ICICS)*, volume 5308 of *Lecture Notes in Computer Science (LNCS)*, pages 33–48. Springer, Berlin/Heidelberg, Germany, October 2008. DOI: 10.1007/978-3-540-88625-9_3. 20

[36] Gerhard P. Hancke and Markus G. Kuhn. An RFID distance bounding protocol. In *Security and Privacy for Emerging Areas in Communications Networks (SecureComm)*, pages 67–73, Washington, DC, USA, September 2005. IEEE. DOI: 10.1109/SECURECOMM.2005.56. 41

[37] C. Helfmeier, C. Boit, D. Nedospasov, and J.-P. Seifert. Cloning physically unclonable functions. In *Hardware-Oriented Security and Trust (HOST)*, pages 1–6, June 2013. DOI: 10.1109/HST.2013.6581556. 17

[38] Anthony Herrewege, Stefan Katzenbeisser, Roel Maes, Roel Peeters, Ahmad-Reza Sadeghi, Ingrid Verbauwhede, and Christian Wachsmann. Reverse fuzzy extractors: Enabling lightweight mutual authentication for PUF-enabled RFIDs. In *Financial Cryptography and Data Security (FC)*, volume 7397 of *Lecture Notes in Computer Science (LNCS)*, pages 374–389. Springer, February 2012. DOI: 10.1007/978-3-642-32946-3_27. 1, 13, 14, 38, 41

[39] Matthew Hoekstra, Reshma Lal, Pradeep Pappachan, Vinay Phegade, and Juan Del Cuvillo. Using innovative instructions to create trustworthy software solutions. In *Workshop on Hardware and Architectural Support for Security and Privacy (HASP)*. ACM, 2013. DOI: 10.1145/2487726.2488370. 1

[40] Daniel Holcomb, Wayne Burleson, and Kevin Fu. Initial SRAM state as a fingerprint and source of true random numbers for RFID tags. In *Workshop on RFID Security (RFIDSec)*. July 2007. 4, 10, 38

[41] Daniel Holcomb, Wayne P. Burleson, and Kevin Fu. Power-up SRAM state as an identifying fingerprint and source of true random numbers. *IEEE Transactions on Computers*, 58(9):1198–1210, September 2009. DOI: 10.1109/TC.2008.212. 16, 23, 24, 27, 29

[42] Daniel E. Holcomb, Amir Rahmati, Mastooreh Salajegheh, Wayne P. Burleson, and Kevin Fu. DRV-fingerprinting: Using data retention voltage of SRAM cells for chip identification. In *Workshop on RFID Security (RFIDSec)*, volume 7739 of *Lecture Notes*

in Computer Science (LNCS), pages 165–179. Springer, July 2013. DOI: 10.1007/978-3-642-36140-1_12. 16

[43] Tanya Ignatenko, Geert-Jan Schrijen, Boris Škorić, Pim Tuyls, and Frans Willems. Estimating the secrecy-rate of physical unclonable functions with the context-tree weighting method. In *IEEE International Symposium on Information Theory (ISIT)*, pages 499–503. IEEE, Washington, DC, USA, July 2006. DOI: 10.1109/ISIT.2006.261765. 23, 27

[44] Intrinsic ID. Product webpage. http://www.intrinsic-id.com/products.htm, January 2013. 3

[45] Markus Jakobsson and Karl-Anders Johansson. Retroactive detection of malware with applications to mobile platforms. In *Workshop on Hot Topics in Security (HotSec)*. USENIX, August 2010. 42

[46] Peter Kampstra. Beanplot: A boxplot alternative for visual comparison of distributions. *Journal of Statistical Software*, 28(1):1–9, October 2008. 30

[47] Deniz Karakoyunlu and Berk Sunar. Differential template attacks on PUF enabled cryptographic devices. In *Workshop on Information Forensics and Security (WIFS)*, pages 1–6. IEEE, Washington, DC, USA, December 2010. DOI: 10.1109/WIFS.2010.5711445. 16

[48] Suleyman Kardas, Mehmet S. Kiraz, Muhammed A. Bingol, and Huseyin Demirci. A novel RFID distance bounding protocol based on physically unclonable functions. In *Radio Frequency Identification: Security and Privacy Issues (RFIDSec)*, volume 7055 of *Lecture Notes in Computer Science (LNCS)*, pages 78–93. Springer, Berlin/Heidelberg, Germany, June 2011. DOI: 10.1007/978-3-642-25286-0_6. 39

[49] Stefan Katzenbeisser, Ünal Kocabaş, Vladimir Rožić, Ahmad-Reza Sadeghi, Ingrid Verbauwhede, and Christian Wachsmann. PUFs: Myth, fact or busted? A security evaluation of physically unclonable functions (PUFs) cast in silicon. In *Cryptographic Hardware and Embedded Systems (CHES)*, volume 7428 of *Lecture Notes in Computer Science (LNCS)*, pages 283–301. Springer, September 2012. DOI: 10.1007/978-3-642-33027-8_17. 17, 23, 27

[50] Stefan Katzenbeisser, Ünal Kocabaş, Vincent van der Leest, Ahmad-Reza Sadeghi, Geert-Jan Schrijen, Heike Schröder, and Christian Wachsmann. Recyclable PUFs: Logically reconfigurable PUFs. In *Workshop on Cryptographic Hardware and Embedded Systems (CHES)*, volume 6917, pages 374–389. Springer, Berlin/Heidelberg, Germany, September 2011. DOI: 10.1007/s13389-011-0016-9. 20

[51] Rick Kennell and Leah H. Jamieson. Establishing the genuinity of remote computer systems. In *USENIX Security Symposium*, pages 21–21, Berkeley, CA, USA, 2003. USENIX Association. 42

[52] Chong H. Kim, Gildas Avoine, François Koeune, François-Xavier Standaert, and Olivier Pereira. The Swiss-Knife RFID distance bounding protocol. In *Information Security and Cryptology (ICISC)*, volume 5461 of *Lecture Notes in Computer Science (LNCS)*, pages 98–115. Springer, Berlin/Heidelberg, Germany, December 2009. 41

[53] Patrick Koeberl, Steffen Schulz, Ahmad-Reza Sadeghi, and Vijay Varadharajan. TrustLite: A security architecture for tiny embedded devices. In *European Conference on Computer Systems (EuroSys)*. ACM, 2014. DOI: 10.1145/2592798.2592824. 1

[54] Oliver Kömmerling and Markus G. Kuhn. Design principles for tamper-resistant smart-card processors. In *USENIX Workshop on Smartcard Technology*, page 2, Berkeley, CA, USA, 1999. USENIX Association. 17

[55] Joonho Kong, Farinaz Koushanfar, Praveen K. Pendyala, Ahmad-Reza Sadeghi, and Christian Wachsmann. PUFatt: Embedded platform attestation based on novel processor-based PUFs. In *Design Automation Conference on Design Automation Conference (DAC)*, pages 1–6, New York, NY, USA, 2014. ACM. DOI: 10.1145/2593069.2593192. 8, 9, 42, 44

[56] Xeno Kovah, Corey Kallenberg, Chris Weathers, Amy Herzog, Matthew Albin, and John Butterworth. New results for Timing-Based attestation. In *IEEE Symposium on Security and Privacy (S&P)*. IEEE, May 2012. DOI: 10.1109/SP.2012.45. 42

[57] S.S. Kumar, J. Guajardo, R. Maes, G.-J. Schrijen, and P. Tuyls. Extended abstract: The butterfly PUF protecting IP on every FPGA. In *Hardware-Oriented Security and Trust, 2008. HOST 2008. IEEE International Workshop on*, pages 67–70, June 2008. DOI: 10.1109/HST.2008.4559053. 3, 4, 11

[58] Klaus Kursawe, Ahmad-Reza Sadeghi, Dries Schellekens, Boris Skoric, and Pim Tuyls. Reconfigurable physical unclonable functions — Enabling technology for tamper-resistant storage. In *Workshop on Hardware-Oriented Security and Trust (HOST)*, pages 22–29. IEEE, Washington, DC, USA, July 2009. DOI: 10.1109/HST.2009.5225058. 20

[59] Jae W. Lee, Daihyun Lim, Blaise Gassend, Edward G. Suh, Marten van Dijk, and Srinivas Devadas. A technique to build a secret key in integrated circuits for identification and authentication applications. In *Symposium on VLSI Circuits*, pages 176–179. IEEE, Washington, DC, USA, June 2004. DOI: 10.1109/VLSIC.2004.1346548. 4, 5, 15, 20, 24, 27

[60] Yanlin Li, Jonathan M. McCune, and Adrian Perrig. VIPER: Verifying the Integrity of PERipherals' firmware. In *ACM Conference on Computer and Communications Security*, pages 3–16. ACM, October 2011. DOI: 10.1145/2046707.2046711. 42

[61] Daihyun Lim. Extracting secret keys from integrated circuits. Master's thesis, Department of Electrical Engineering and Computer Science, Massachusetts Institute of Technology (MIT), June 2004. 4, 5, 20, 27

[62] Daihyun Lim, Jae W. Lee, Blaise Gassend, Edward G. Suh, Marten van Dijk, and Srinivas Devadas. Extracting secret keys from integrated circuits. *IEEE Transactions on Very Large Scale Integration (VLSI) Systems*, 13(10):1200–1205, October 2005. DOI: 10.1109/TVLSI.2005.859470. 3, 12, 20, 39, 55, 61, 62

[63] Lang Lin, Dan Holcomb, Dilip K. Krishnappa, Prasad Shabadi, and Wayne Burleson. Low-power sub-threshold design of secure physical unclonable functions. In *International Symposium on Low-Power Electronics and Design (ISLPED)*, pages 43–48. IEEE, Washington, DC, USA, August 2010. DOI: 10.1145/1840845.1840855. 4, 15

[64] Roel Maes. An accurate probabilistic reliability model for silicon PUFs. In *Cryptographic Hardware and Embedded Systems (CHES)*, volume 8086 of *Lecture Notes in Computer Science (LNCS)*, pages 73–89. Springer, Berlin/Heidelberg, Germany, 2013. DOI: 10.1007/978-3-642-40349-1_5. 62

[65] Roel Maes, Pim Tuyls, and Ingrid Verbauwhede. Intrinsic PUFs from flip-flops on reconfigurable devices. In *Benelux Workshop on Information and System Security*. November 2008. 4, 7, 11, 24

[66] Roel Maes and Ingrid Verbauwhede. Physically unclonable functions: A study on the state of the art and future research directions. In *Towards Hardware-Intrinsic Security*, Information Security and Cryptography, pages 3–37. Springer, Berlin/Heidelberg, Germany, November 2010. DOI: 10.1007/978-3-642-14452-3_1. 1, 3, 5, 7, 12, 20, 25, 27, 29

[67] Abhranil Maiti, Jeff Casarona, Luke McHale, and Patrick Schaumont. A large scale characterization of RO-PUF. In *Symposium on Hardware-Oriented Security and Trust (HOST)*, pages 94–99. IEEE, Washington, DC, USA, June 2010. 4

[68] M. Majzoobi, M. Rostami, F. Koushanfar, D.S. Wallach, and S. Devadas. Slender PUF protocol: A lightweight, robust, and secure authentication by substring matching. In *Security and Privacy Workshops (SPW)*, pages 33–44, May 2012. DOI: 10.1109/SPW.2012.30. 9

[69] Mehrdad Majzoobi, Farinaz Koushanfar, and Miodrag Potkonjak. Lightweight secure PUFs. In *International Conference on Computer-Aided Design (ICCAD)*, pages 670–673. IEEE, Washington, DC, USA, November 2008. DOI: 10.1109/ICCAD.2008.4681648. 15

[70] Mehrdad Majzoobi, Farinaz Koushanfar, and Miodrag Potkonjak. Testing techniques for hardware security. In *International Test Conference (ITC)*, pages 1–10. IEEE, Washington, DC, USA, October 2008. DOI: 10.1109/TEST.2008.4700636. 5, 15

[71] Mehrdad Majzoobi, Farinaz Koushanfar, and Miodrag Potkonjak. Techniques for design and implementation of secure reconfigurable PUFs. *ACM Transactions on Reconfigurable Technology and Systems (TRETS)*, 2(1):1–33, March 2009. DOI: 10.1145/1502781.1502786. 5, 6, 15, 20

[72] George Marsaglia. The Marsaglia random number CDROM including the diehard battery of tests of randomness. `http://www.stat.fsu.edu/pub/diehard/`, April 2013. 27

[73] Frank McKeen, Ilya Alexandrovich, Alex Berenzon, Carlos V. Rozas, Hisham Shafi, Vedvyas Shanbhogue, and Uday R. Savagaonkar. Innovative instructions and software model for isolated execution. In *Workshop on Hardware and Architectural Support for Security and Privacy (HASP)*. ACM, 2013. DOI: 10.1145/2487726.2488368. 1

[74] Dominik Merli, Dieter Schuster, Frederic Stumpf, and Georg Sigl. Side-channel analysis of PUFs and fuzzy extractors. In *Trust and Trustworthy Computing (TRUST)*, volume 6740 of *Lecture Notes in Computer Science (LNCS)*, pages 33–47. Springer, Berlin/Heidelberg, Germany, June 2011. DOI: 10.1007/978-3-642-21599-5_3. 16

[75] Yannick Monnet, Marc Renaudin, and Regis Leveugle. Designing resistant circuits against malicious faults injection using asynchronous logic. *IEEE Trans. Comput.*, 55:1104–1115, September 2006. DOI: 10.1109/TC.2006.143. 21

[76] National Institute of Standards and Technology (NIST). Announcing the advanced eencryption standard (AES). Federal Information Processing Standards Publication 197, `http://csrc.nist.gov/publications/fips/fips197/fips-197.pdf`, 2001. 24, 63

[77] D. Nedospasov, J.-P. Seifert, C. Helfmeier, and C. Boit. Invasive PUF analysis. In *Fault Diagnosis and Tolerance in Cryptography (FDTC)*, pages 30–38, Aug 2013. DOI: 10.1109/FDTC.2013.19. 17

[78] Jr. Nick L. Petroni, Timothy Fraser, Jesus Molina, and William A. Arbaugh. Copilot — A coprocessor-based kernel runtime integrity monitor. In *USENIX Security Symposium*, pages 179–194. USENIX, August 2004. 42

[79] Job Noorman, Pieter Agten, Wilfried Daniels, Raoul Strackx, Anthony Van Herrewege, Christophe Huygens, Bart Preneel, Ingrid Verbauwhede, and Frank Piessens. Sancus: Low-cost trustworthy extensible networked devices with a zero-software trusted computing base. In *USENIX Security Symposium*. USENIX Association, 2013. 1

[80] NXP Semiconductors N.V. NXP strengthens SmartMX2 security chips with PUF anti-cloning technology, February 2013. 3

[81] Yossef Oren, Ahmad-Reza Sadeghi, and Christian Wachsmann. On the effectiveness of the remanence decay side-channel to clone memory-based PUFs. In *Workshop on Cryptographic Hardware and Embedded Systems (CHES)*, volume 8086 of *Lecture Notes in Computer Science (LNCS)*, pages 107–125. Springer, Berlin/Heidelberg, Germany, August 2013. DOI: 10.1007/978-3-642-40349-1_7. 16

[82] Emmanuel Owusu, Jorge Guajardo, Jonathan McCune, Jim Newsome, Adrian Perrig, and Amit Vasudevan. OASIS: On achieving a sanctuary for integrity and secrecy on untrusted platforms. In *ACM Conference on Computer & Communications Security (CCS)*. ACM, 2013. DOI: 10.1145/2508859.2516678. 1

[83] Erdinç Öztürk, Ghaith Hammouri, and Berk Sunar. Towards robust low cost authentication for pervasive devices. In *Conference on Pervasive Computing and Communications (PerCom)*, pages 170–178. IEEE, Washington, DC, USA, March 2008. DOI: 10.1109/PERCOM.2008.54. 1, 3, 4, 15, 20

[84] Ravikanth Pappu, Ben Recht, Jason Taylor, and Neil Gershenfeld. Physical one-way functions. *Science*, 297(5589):2026–2030, September 2002. DOI: 10.1126/science.1074376. 1, 3, 47

[85] Bryan Parno, Jonathan M. McCune, and Adrian Perrig. Bootstrapping trust in commodity computers. In *IEEE Symposium on Security and Privacy (S&P)*, pages 414–429. IEEE, May 2010. DOI: 10.1109/SP.2010.32. 41

[86] Pedro Peris-Lopez, Julio C. Hernandez-Castro, Juan M. E. Tapiador, Esther Palomar, and Jan C. A. van der Lubbe. Cryptographic puzzles and distance-bounding protocols: Practical tools for RFID security. In *IEEE International Conference on RFID*, pages 45–52. IEEE, April 2010. DOI: 10.1109/RFID.2010.5467258. 41

[87] Krzysztof Pietrzak. A Leakage-Resilient mode of operation. In *Advances in Cryptology (EUROCRYPT)*, volume 5479 of *Lecture Notes in Computer Science (LNCS)*, pages 462–482. Springer, April 2009. DOI: 10.1007/978-3-642-01001-9_27. 57

[88] Reinhard Posch. Protecting devices by active coating. *Journal of Universal Computer Science*, 4(7):652–668, July 1998. 17, 62

[89] Damith C. Ranasinghe, Daniel W. Engels, and Peter H Cole. Security and privacy: Modest proposals for low-cost RFID systems. In *Auto-ID Labs Research Workshop*. September 2004. 3, 37, 38

[90] Kasper B. Rasmussen and Srdjan Čapkun. Realization of RF distance bounding. In *USENIX Conference on Security*, page 25, Berkeley, CA, USA, December 2010. USENIX Association. 41

[91] Pappu Ravikanth. *Physical One-Way Functions*. Ph.D. thesis, Massachusetts Institute of Technology, 77 Massachusetts Avenue, Cambridge, MA 02139-4307, USA, March 2001. ix, 47

[92] Ulrich Rührmair. SIMPL systems: On a public key variant of physical unclonable functions. Cryptology ePrint Archive, Report 2009/255, June 2009. 19

[93] Ulrich Rührmair. SIMPL systems, or: Can we design cryptographic hardware without secret key information? In *Current Trends in Theory and Practice of Computer Science (SOF-SEM)*, volume 6543 of *Lecture Notes in Computer Science (LNCS)*, pages 26–45. Springer, Berlin/Heidelberg, Germany, January 2011.

[94] Ulrich Rührmair, Qingqing Chen, Martin Stutzmann, Paolo Lugli, Ulf Schlichtmann, and György Csaba. Towards electrical, integrated implementations of SIMPL systems. In *Workshop on Information Security Theory and Practices (WISTP)*, volume 6033 of *Lecture Notes in Computer Science (LNCS)*, pages 277–292. Springer, Berlin/Heidelberg, Germany, April 2010. DOI: 10.1007/978-3-642-12368-9_22. 19, 20

[95] Ulrich Rührmair, Frank Sehnke, Jan Sölter, Gideon Dror, Srinivas Devadas, and Jürgen Schmidhuber. Modeling attacks on physical unclonable functions. In *ACM Conference on Computer and Communications Security (CCS)*, pages 237–249. ACM, New York, NY, USA, October 2010. DOI: 10.1145/1866307.1866335. 5, 6, 7, 15, 32

[96] Ulrich Rührmair, Jan Sölter, and Frank Sehnke. On the foundations of physical unclonable functions. Cryptology ePrint Archive, Report 2009/277, June 2009. 5, 6, 47, 48

[97] Ulrich Rührmair and Marten van Dijk. PUFs in security protocols: Attack models and security evaluations. In *IEEE Symposium on Security and Privacy (S&P)*, pages 286–300, Washington, DC, USA, 2013. IEEE Computer Society. DOI: 10.1109/SP.2013.27. 61

[98] Andrew Rukhin, Juan Soto, James Nechvatal, Miles Smid, Elaine Barker, Stefan Leigh, Mark Levenson, Mark Vangel, David Banks, Alan Heckert, James Dray, and San Vo. A statistical test suite for random and pseudorandom number generators for cryptographic applications. Special Publication 800-22 Revision 1a, NIST, April 2010. 27

[99] Ahmad-Reza Sadeghi, Ivan Visconti, and Christian Wachsmann. Enhancing RFID security and privacy by physically unclonable functions. In *Towards Hardware-Intrinsic Security*, Information Security and Cryptography, pages 281–305. Springer, Berlin/Heidelberg, Germany, November 2010. DOI: 10.1007/978-3-642-14452-3_13. 3, 37, 39

[100] Ahmad-Reza Sadeghi, Ivan Visconti, and Christian Wachsmann. PUF-enhanced RFID security and privacy. In *Secure Component and System Identification (SECSI)*. April 2010. DOI: 10.1016/j.jnca.2012.08.006. 1

[101] Nitesh Saxena and Jonathan Voris. We can remember it for you wholesale: Implications of data remanence on the use of RAM for true random number generation on RFID tags (RFIDSec 2009). July 2009. 16

[102] Dries Schellekens, Brecht Wyseur, and Bart Preneel. Remote attestation on legacy operating systems with Trusted Platform Modules. *Sci. Comput. Program.*, 74(1-2):13–22, 2008. DOI: 10.1016/j.scico.2008.09.005. 42

[103] Steffen Schulz, Ahmad-Reza Sadeghi, and Christian Wachsmann. Short paper: Lightweight remote attestation using physical functions. In *ACM Conference on Wireless Network Security (WiSec)*, pages 109–114. ACM, New York, NY, USA, June 2011. DOI: 10.1145/1998412.1998432. 3, 42, 44

[104] Georgios Selimis, Mario Konijnenburg, Maryam Ashouei, Jos Huisken, Harmke de Groot, Vicnent van der Leest, Geert-Jan Schrijen, M. van Hulst, and P. Tuyls. Evaluation of 90nm 6T-SRAM as physical unclonable function for secure key generation in wireless sensor nodes. In *IEEE International Symposium on Circuits and Systems (ISCAS)*, pages 567–570. IEEE, Washington, DC, USA, May 2011. DOI: 10.1109/ISCAS.2011.5937628. 16

[105] Arvind Seshadri, Mark Luk, Adrian Perrig, Leendert van Doorn, and Pradeep Khosla. SCUBA: Secure code update by attestation in sensor networks. In *ACM Workshop on Wireless Security (WiSe)*, pages 85–94, New York, NY, USA, 2006. ACM. DOI: 10.1145/1161289.1161306. 42, 44

[106] Arvind Seshadri, Mark Luk, Elaine Shi, Adrian Perrig, Leendert van Doorn, and Pradeep Khosla. Pioneer: Verifying integrity and guaranteeing execution of code on legacy platforms. In *Symposium on Operating Systems Principles (SOSP)*, pages 1–16. ACM, October 2005. DOI: 10.1145/1095809.1095812. 42

[107] Umesh Shankar, Monica Chew, and J. D. Tygar. Side effects are not sufficient to authenticate software. In *USENIX Security Symposium*, page 7. USENIX, August 2004. 42

[108] Saloomeh Shariati, François Koeune, and François-Xavier Standaert. Security analysis of image-based PUFs for anti-counterfeiting. In *Communications and Multimedia Security*, volume 7394 of *Lecture Notes in Computer Science (LNCS)*, pages 26–38. Springer, September 2012. DOI: 10.1007/978-3-642-32805-3_3. 48, 59

[109] Saloomeh Shariati, François-Xavier Standaert, Laurent Jacques, and Benoit Macq. Analysis and experimental evaluation of image-based PUFs. 2(3):189–206, October 2012. DOI: 10.1007/s13389-012-0041-3. 48, 59

[110] Dave Singelée and Bart Preneel. Distance bounding in noisy environments. In *Security and Privacy in Ad-hoc and Sensor Networks*, volume 4572 of *Lecture Notes in Computer Science (LNCS)*, pages 101–115. Springer, Berlin/Heidelberg, Germany, July 2007. DOI: 10.1007/978-3-540-73275-4_8. 41

[111] Sergei Skorobogatov. Semi-invasive attacks — A new approach to hardware security analysis. Technical Report UCAM-CL-TR-630, University of Cambridge, 15 JJ Thomson Avenue, Cambridge CB03 0FD, UK, April 2005. 20

[112] Sergei Skorobogatov. Local heating attacks on Flash memory devices. In *IEEE International Workshop on Hardware-Oriented Security and Trust (HOST'09)*, pages 1–6. IEEE, July 27 2009. DOI: 10.1109/HST.2009.5225028. 20, 21

[113] Raoul Strackx, Frank Piessens, and Bart Preneel. Efficient isolation of trusted subsystems in embedded systems. In *Security and Privacy in Communication Networks*, volume 50 of *Lecture Notes of the Institute for Computer Sciences, Social Informatics and Telecommunications Engineering*. Springer, 2010. DOI: 10.1007/978-3-642-16161-2_20. 1

[114] Ying Su, Jeremy Holleman, and Brian P Otis. A 1.6pJ/bit 96% stable chip-ID generating circuit using process variations. In *International Solid-State Circuits Conference (ISSCC)*, pages 406–611. IEEE, Washington, DC, USA, February 2007. DOI: 10.1109/ISSCC.2007.373466. 11, 27

[115] Ying Su, Jeremy Holleman, and Brian P Otis. A digital 1.6 pJ/bit chip identification circuit using process variations. *IEEE Journal of Solid-State Circuits*, 43(1):69–77, January 2008. DOI: 10.1109/JSSC.2007.910961. 4, 24

[116] Edward G. Suh and Srinivas Devadas. Physical unclonable functions for device authentication and secret key generation. In *ACM/IEEE Design Automation Conference (DAC)*, pages 9–14. IEEE, Washington, DC, USA, June 2007. DOI: 10.1145/1278480.1278484. 4, 7, 8, 24, 27

[117] G. Edward Suh, Dwaine Clarke, Blaise Gassend, Marten van Dijk, and Srinivas Devadas. AEGIS: Architecture for tamper-evident and tamper-resistant processing. In *International Conference on Supercomputing (ICS)*. ACM, 2003. DOI: 10.1145/782814.782838. 1

[118] Christopher Tarnovsky. Hacking the smartcard chip. Blackhat DC 2010, February 2010. 17

[119] Carlos Tokunaga, David T. Blaauw, and Trevor N. Mudge. True random number generator with a metastability-based quality control. In *IEEE International Solid-State Circuits Conference (ISSCC)*, pages 404–611. IEEE, Washington, DC, USA, February 2007. DOI: 10.1109/JSSC.2007.910965. 16

[120] Trusted Computing Group (TCG). TPM main specification, March 2011. 42, 64

[121] Trusted Computing Group (TCG). Website. http://www.trustedcomputinggroup.org, 2011. 1

[122] Pim Tuyls and Lejla Batina. RFID-tags for anti-counterfeiting. In *Topics in Cryptology (CT-RSA)*, volume 3860 of *Lecture Notes in Computer Science (LNCS)*, pages 115–131. Springer, Berlin/Heidelberg, Germany, February 2006. DOI: 10.1007/11605805_8. 1, 3, 37, 39, 55, 61, 62

[123] Pim Tuyls, Geert-Jan Schrijen, Boris Škorić, Jan van Geloven, Nynke Verhaegh, and Rob Wolters. Read-proof hardware from protective coatings. In *Cryptographic Hardware and Embedded Systems (CHES)*, volume 4249 of *Lecture Notes in Computer Science (LNCS)*, pages 369–383. Springer, Berlin/Heidelberg, Germany, October 2006. DOI: 10.1007/11894063_29. 4, 12, 17, 27, 62

[124] Pim Tuyls, Boris Škorić, Tanya Ignatenko, Frans Willems, and Geert-Jan Schrijen. Entropy estimation for optical PUFs based on context-tree weighting methods. In *Security with Noisy Data*, pages 217–233. Springer, London, UK, October 2007. DOI: 10.1007/978-1-84628-984-2. 23, 27

[125] Pim Tuyls, Boris Škorić, Sjoerd Stallinga, Anton H. M. Akkermans, and Wil Ophey. Information-theoretic security analysis of physical uncloneable functions. In *Financial Cryptography and Data Security (FC)*, volume 3570 of *Lecture Notes in Computer Science (LNCS)*, page 578. Springer, Berlin/Heidelberg, Germany, February 2005. DOI: 10.1007/11507840_15. 23, 27

[126] Robbert van den Berg, Boris Skoric, and Vincent van der Leest. Bias-based modeling and entropy analysis of PUFs. Cryptology ePrint Archive, Report 2013/656, October 2013. 17

[127] Vincent van der Leest, Geert-Jan Schrijen, Helena Handschuh, and Pim Tuyls. Hardware intrinsic security from D flip-flops. In *ACM Workshop on Scalable Trusted Computing (STC)*, pages 53–62. ACM, New York, NY, USA, October 2010. DOI: 10.1145/1867635.1867644. 4, 11, 23, 27

[128] Verayo Inc. Product webpage. http://www.verayo.com/product/products.html, January 2013. 3

[129] Boris Škorić, Stefan Maubach, Tom Kevenaar, and Pim Tuyls. Information-theoretic analysis of capacitive physical unclonable functions. *Journal of Applied Physics*, 100(2):024902–024902–11, July 2006. DOI: 10.1063/1.2209532. 17, 23, 62

[130] Boris Škorić, Stefan Maubach, Tom Kevenaar, and Pim Tuyls. Information-theoretic analysis of coating PUFs. Cryptology ePrint Archive, Report 2006/101, March 2006. 23

[131] Boris Škorić, Pim Tuyls, and Wil Ophey. Robust key extraction from physical uncloneable functions. In *Applied Cryptography and Network Security (ACNS)*, volume 3531 of *Lecture Notes in Computer Science (LNCS)*, pages 99–135. Springer, Berlin/Heidelberg, Germany, June 2005. DOI: 10.1007/11496137_28. 3, 12, 39, 55, 61, 62

[132] Yinglei Wang, Wing kei Yu, Shuo Wu, G. Malysa, G.E. Suh, and E.C. Kan. Flash memory for ubiquitous hardware security functions: True random number generation and device fingerprints. In *Security and Privacy (SP), 2012 IEEE Symposium on*, pages 33–47, May 2012. DOI: 10.1109/SP.2012.12. 11

[133] Christian Wachsmann. *Trusted and Privacy-preserving Embedded Systems: Advances in Design, Analysis and Application of Lightweight Privacy-preserving Authentication and Physical Security Primitives*. Ph.D. thesiss, Technische Universität Darmstadt, Darmstadt, March 2014. ix

[134] Frans Willems, Yuri M. Shtarkov, and Tjalling J Tjalkens. The context-tree weighting method: Basic properties. *IEEE Transactions on Information Theory*, 41(3):653–664, May 1995. DOI: 10.1109/18.382012. 27, 63

[135] Johannes Winter. Trusted computing building blocks for embedded Linux-based ARM TrustZone platforms. In *ACM Workshop on Scalable Trusted Computing (STC)*. ACM, 2008. DOI: 10.1145/1456455.1456460. 1

[136] Yi Yang, Xinran Wang, Sencun Zhu, and Guohong Cao. Distributed software-based attestation for node compromise detection in sensor networks. In *Symposium on Reliable Distributed Systems (SRDS)*, 2007. DOI: 10.1109/SRDS.2007.31. 44

Authors' Biographies

CHRISTIAN WACHSMANN

Christian Wachsmann is a postdoctoral researcher at the Intel Collaborative Research Institute for Secure Computing (ICRI-SC) at TU Darmstadt. He received his Ph.D. in computer science from Technische Universität Darmstadt, Germany. His current research focuses on the design, development, formal modeling, and security analysis of security architectures and cryptographic protocols to verify the software integrity (attestation) of embedded systems. Christian is the main author of more than 30 scientific publications in internationally renowned journals and conferences on information and communications security.

AHMAD-REZA SADEGHI

Ahmad-Reza Sadeghi is a full professor of computer science at Technische Universität Darmstadt, Germany. He is the head of the System Security Lab at the Center for Advanced Security Research Darmstadt (CASED) and Director of the Intel Collaborative Research Institute for Secure Computing (ICRI-SC) at TU Darmstadt. He holds a Ph.D. in computer science from the University of Saarland in Saarbrücken, Germany. Prior to academia, he worked in research and development of telecommunications enterprises, such as Ericsson Telecommunications. He has served on the Editorial Board of the ACM Transactions on Information and System Security.

Printed in the United States
by Baker & Taylor Publisher Services